Fare
Vo

CW00539781

BEDFORD BUSES
OF THE
1930S AND 1940S

Alan Earnshaw

Trans-Pennine Publishing

CONTENTS

Front Cover: *This superbly restored Country Bus, now preserved in Jersey carries a Churchill body on a WS chassis. This vehicle was built as an estate bus but later worked for a time at Pentonville Prison.*

Rear Cover Top: *The most famous of all Bedford buses, which is also shown on the page opposite, is the pioneer WHB/Waveney TM 9347. Seen in a Vauxhall publicity picture in 1981, the coach looks in pristine condition despite its 50 years of age.*

Rear Cover Bottom: *Below an advertisement for 'K Shoes' at the Garret in Lerwick, a Shetland Islands OB awaits its next trip to Reawick. Then in service with Watts of Reawick, HGE 219 is now preserved by Moulds of Reading.*

Title Page: *Heading along the A23, London - Brighton road, this OB from Margos Coaches is pictured crossing the Downs in a superb setting. This is one of the delightful pictures that captures the feel of post-war motoring in Britain, and brings back memories of happy day trips and holiday excursions.*

This Page: *On 31st December 1936 a Bedford WTB with an un-identified body (CJH 157), works on the Luton - Kimpton service of Enterprise Motors.*

The **Nostalgia Road** Series ™
is conceived, designed and published
by
Trans-Pennine Publishing Ltd.
PO Box 10
Appleby-in-Westmorland
Cumbria, CA16 6FA
Tel. 017683 51053
Fax. 017683 53558
ISDN. 017683 53684
e-mail trans.pennine@virgin.net
(A Quality Guild registered company)

Reprographics
Barnabus Design & Repro
Threemilestone, Truro
Cornwall, TR4 9AN
01872 241185

And Printed in Cumbria by
Kent Valley Colour Printers Ltd.
Shap Road Industrial Estate
Kendal, Cumbria LA9 6NZ
01539 741344

And Produced In Conjunction With
Vauxhall Heritage

ISBN 1 903016 22 3
British Cataloguing in Publication Data
A catalogue record for this book is available from the British Library

Introduction

When I was given the opportunity to examine the Vauxhall photographic archive, I was astounded by the wealth of material on Bedford buses and coaches that had been deposited away over the years. It was therefore with very great pleasure that I felt able to suggest to the company that we produce a series of three books detailing the history of Bedford buses. Thankfully that suggestion was adopted, and I am delighted to offer the first ever official book on Bedford buses.

As the co-owner of a pair of Bedford coaches (a 1951 SB and a 1965 VAS), this is something of an added bonus, for I have also been highly privileged to look at the written archives, including official records, period sales literature, operating handbooks, workshop manuals, and the full set of *The Bedford Transport Magazine* issues. In so doing I have been able to go right back to original source material, and look at the documented progression of Bedford bus and coach development. Some of what I have to say in the pages that follow may seem to be at variance with what others have written before, and this may 'set the cat amongst the pigeons'. However, I have had to go through several sets of original material to ascertain exactly what the correction position has been, as for example the date when Plaxtons began bodying Bedford chassis.

Above: *One of the most famous Bedford coaches, is this WHB with a Waveney body which left the factory on 31st August 1931, and was delivered to local operator John Woodham of Melchbourne. It ran local trips for his company for many years, where it became known as the 'Melchbourne Flyer'. However, it is also known to have done excursions to exotic locations like Skegness and Great Yarmouth. It was eventually purchased for preservation by local Bedford dealers Arlington Motors, and is now part of the Vauxhall Heritage Collection at Luton.*

The pictures used in this publication, and the two that follow, are all official Bedford images, and because of this it may seem that there is a distinct prejudice against coachbuilders like Plaxton, Harrington, and so on, for the preponderance of images show Bedford-Duple combinations. Yet that is exactly what the official archive reflects, and for the simple reason that the Bedford-Duple combination accounted for a massive slice of the British coach scene during the years covered in these books. I therefore make no excuse for relying entirely on the Vauxhall archive for, as I am sure you will agree, it contains images of stunning historical value. I for one am delighted to have had insight into this wonderful collection, and I hope you will agree with our choice of illustrations.

Alan Earnshaw,   Appleby, August 2000

3

The WHB and WLB Series

It has to be said that there is quite a good deal of confusion surrounding the earlier Bedford bus chassis production, and there is often a mistaken impression that the earlier Bedford models were nothing more than 'badge engineering' of British-built Chevrolets.

It is true that the American influence was heavy in the early models, Vauxhall having become part of General Motors (the owners of Chevrolet) in 1925. Chevrolet also had its own British plant at Hendon as well as having some vehicles built at Luton. On this point Vauxhall's own brochure on their bus history pointed out: 'Certainly British-built Chevrolets had been produced at the Luton factory since 1929. Just as certainly there were distinct differences between the new Bedfords and their earlier cousins, similar though they may have been in looks.' So, what are the real facts?

Firstly, by the end of 1931 Bedfords were the only commercial vehicles being built at Luton and the basis for the forthcoming bus production was the new 2-ton commercial vehicle chassis! It is also clear that in introducing it, Vauxhall definitely had its mind on producing something for the rapidly emerging small bus market. In the latter part of 1929 small bus chassis such as Morris Commercial,

Above: *Few readers will appreciate that London Transport had any Bedfords in its fleet, but here we see a WLB (PJ 8430). This was probably bought during the time LT were evaluating 'small' buses to replace the hotch-potch of models it had acquired from private operators and before it standardised on the Leyland Cub.*

Dennis and Gilford were acquired for 'comparative evaluation' at Luton, thus indicating that Vauxhall were aiming at something more than a modified Chevrolet. The differences between Chevrolet and the new Bedford 2-tonners were mainly mechanical, significantly in the chassis construction, the rear wheels and axles, and in the engine lubricating systems.

It is known that the first buses were made on the truck chassis, and two coaches (one with a Jennings body and one with a Rainforth body) were made before the WHB and WLB bus chassis were properly introduced. However, as one of the pictures on page 6 shows, the first Bedford passenger vehicle chassis looked nothing at all like a bus. The picture was shown in a General Motors publication dated May 1931, and the notes on the back of the original General Motors print inform us that the vehicle was, 'a new type of Bedford coach chassis constructed to carry miners to and from the colliery.'

The specifications for the two new bus chassis were identical, but the major difference was the wheelbase, for that on the WHB was 131 inches (3.32m), whilst the WLB was 157 inches (3.98m), and this gave them a potential seating capacity of 14 or 20 respectively. From the outset Vauxhall recognised that the demand would be for the larger of the two models, so it aimed the bulk of its promotional activity towards the WLB. Indeed, the WHB was to be a very short-lived model, for in April 1932 Vauxhall introduced a variant of the 12cwt VYC/VXC chassis for light bus work, and they phased out the WHB. The last WHB chassis (No. 100103) was turned out in the Spring of 1933 with 102 being built in total. The WLB would run for another two years, and when the last of these (No.110133) ran down the line in April 1935, a total of 1,892 had been built.

The chassis was made from pressed steel channel section with a depth of 7 inches (178mm) and a thickness of $7/32$ of an inch (5.5mm) and generally both models had six cross members, although some WHBs had just five cross members but don't ask me the reason behind this! Beyond the fifth cross member the chassis curved up to a slight arch where it passed over the rear axle, then at the sixth cross member the frame began to taper down to the end of the chassis where the section was about $4^1/2$ inches (114mm) deep. At the tail of the chassis, two underslung cross brackets formed a cradle to carry the spare wheel. The rear springs were mounted on hanging plates on the outside of the chassis frame, directly opposite the fifth and sixth cross members. These springs were made of silico-manganese steel and were 54 inches (1.37m) in length and $2^1/2$ inches (63.5mm) wide. The 16 leaves were designed to give progressive action as the load increased; ensuring maximum comfort at all times whatever the load being carried

Mounted on the offside of the chassis, roughly between the third and fourth cross members, was the 20-gallon (90.9 litre) petrol tank, which was housed in a sheet steel frame. The petrol tap was fitted with an extension handle so that the supply could be cut off on the outside of the vehicle. Lifting petrol to the Zenith 'Down Draught' carburettor was achieved by means of a pump driven by the camshaft.

Between the first and second cross members, the front of the vehicle was fitted with an engine cowl made from sheet steel, with louvred 'lift off' plates on either side. The curved bonnet top could be detached for ease of maintenance, but ordinarily it was in a 'fixed' position. A chrome-plated radiator grill and surround, with filler cap finished off the engine cover, whilst pressed steel wings covered the front wheels. The rear of the engine cowl had a special 'bus-type' dashboard, whilst the front end of the chassis had a twin bar bumper in chrome finish. Large headlamps were mounted on a cross bar that spanned the front of the radiator grill, whilst sidelights were mounted on top of the wings. There was no scuttle as would become normal practice on later Bedfords, so all the bodywork to the rear of the engine side plates had to be provided by the operator's chosen coachbuilder. The total weight of the WLB chassis was $32^3/4$ cwt (1663.7kg); it had a 9 inch (228.6mm) road clearance at the lowest point, and a turning circle of 342 inch (8.68m).

Above: *In the collection of photographs, I found quite a few 'quirky' images and a few guaranteed to raise a smile. For example, this 'Travelling Laxative Demonstration' team, run by 'E-Lax' (the makers of a chocolate laxative), toured the British Isles in a Bedford WLB with a Duple body.*

Below: *Not quite a Bedford double-decker, for this was a travelling hotel operated by Peter Crerar of Crieff. It was built in Scotland in 1933, and had three bedrooms on the upper deck, and a saloon and kitchen on the lower deck. It a had crew of two (a driver and a chef) who both slept in the cab. The cost of full board was £1 per person per day - a real busman's holiday perhaps!*

Top Left: *It may not look like it , but this is probably the first ever Bedford bus. It was made with a convertible body to carry both miners or freight, by The North Worcestershire Garage of Stourbridge. They used a Bedford long wheel base chassis, and made it so that it could be quickly and easily converted into a rigid tilt lorry. The seating capacity was 20 persons, carried ten each side on transverse benches.*

Centre Left: *This rare Great Western Railway/Bedford publicity picture shows the new 'inter-city' air-links that the Railway Air Services started to promote in 1932. The aeroplane G-AAGW is a three-engined Westland Wessex, which carried six passengers between Cardiff and Plymouth. Providing the airport-city link, is a 20-seat WLB, with a 'Sun Saloon' body. It is seen with an advert on the windows stating a complete purchase price of £590, about £36,250 at today's prices.*

Bottom Left: *This Waveney advert shows a price of £280 (£17,208), but this was not an inclusive price and the chassis cost extra*

Underneath the cowl, there was a powerful 6-cylinder 3177cc engine giving 44bhp at 2400rpm, which was rated by the RAC as 26.33hp. But towards the end of production, and just ahead of the WTB, the power unit was described as 'a 27hp engine developing 64bhp at 2,800 rpm. It had a bore of $3^5/16$ inches (84.14mm) and a stroke of $3^3/4$ inches (95.25mm) with accessible overhead valves'.

A major difference from the Chevrolet engines was the rigid four-bearing crankshaft drop-forged from high tensile steel, which had been statically and dynamically tested and was thus far more reliable than the American designed crankshaft. It also featured full pressure automatic force-feed lubrication (by means of a gear-type pump in the sump driven by an inclined shaft from the camshaft), crankcase ventilation and a cartridge type oil filter. In this new arrangement, the connecting rod big ends had been 'drilled out' to force lubricants to the cylinder bores at every revolution of the crankshaft.

Transmission was by a 4-speed gearbox with large bearings, rolled gear teeth and an extra low first gear. The gear ratios were 6.2:1 in top, 10.6:1 in third, 21.5:1 in second and 44.8:1 in first; reverse was 44.3:1. A one-piece open tubular prop shaft, with Hardy Spicer universal joints and needle roller bearings, provided drive to the rear axle. This was a fully floating unit with a one-piece cast steel housing, like those used in the Bedford trucks, with an initial ratio of 5.8 :1 but later increasing to 6.2:1. In the later models the rear axle was modified slightly, and set at an angle of 45 degrees, whilst the bevel pinion was straddled to give better tooth contact.

All the ordinarily inaccessible lubrication points, were connected by connecting pipe lines to a series of grouped greasers, which in turn were fed by a Tecalemite high-pressure oil gun. The front axle was of the 'Reverse Elliott' type from 'I' beam section located by inclined pivot pins. Taper roller bearings were fitted on the front hubs, whilst plain thrust bearings were used to carry the load on the stub axle.

The brakes also saw substantial improvement from the Chevrolet trucks, but the parentage of the braking system was still obvious. The foot brakes operated on all four wheels, but the same brake shoes could also be operated by the handbrake. The front brake drums were 12$\frac{1}{2}$ inches (317.5mm) with a 2-inch (50.8mm) wide lining; the rear brakes were 16 inch (406.4mm) in diameter with a 2$\frac{1}{2}$ inch (63.5mm) wide lining. The brake system was later improved by the addition of a powerful Dewandre Vacuum Servo Cylinder, which was again introduced late in 1934 ahead of the introduction of the WTB chassis. Steering was by worm and wheel, with a ratio of 15:1. The wheels were pierced steel wheel discs, which were detachable at the hub. The tyres were 32x6TT 8-ply, although heavy duty tyres could be supplied as an extra at £16 (£983.04). A mechanical tyre pump was mounted on the near side of the gearbox, and this was operated by a small hand lever. This pumped air through a small conditioning bottle (to extract any oil or water vapour) to a nozzle on the dashboard.

The 12-volt electrical equipment was by Lucas and was powered by two Exide 6v (Type 2/3-XC15-1M) batteries wired in series. A CAV generator of constant voltage ensured batteries were kept in charge, with the rate of charge varying up on the demand being placed on the system. A multiple fuse box was another new innovation on the Bedford coach chassis, as was a floor-mounted headlamp dip switch. A combined tail-stop lamp was fitted on the end of the chassis, but these were invariably relocated into the body panels by the various coachbuilders. The cost of the MoT 'approved' chassis were £250 (£15,360) for the WHB and £265 (£16,281) for the WLB.

Because of the proximity of Vauxhall's Sales & Service Depot, in Edgware Road, The Hyde (London NW9), to Duple Bodies & Motors, this Hendon firm thus became the official builders for the new Bedfords. Their first offerings were a bus at £550 (£33,792) and the Sun Saloon at £590 (£36,249), but these prices were soon set to fall as we will see. However, Duple were not alone in offering bodies for the new Bedford, as the firm of Waveney from Oulton Broad were appointed as official builders. It has been written that the two other official builders on the chassis were Grose of Northampton and Rainforth at Lincoln, but we know that the well-known coachbuilders J. H. Jennings of Sandbach were also officially approved builders.

Top Right: *A big debate in the 1930s was on the size of bus needed to 'open up' country areas, and the Ministry of Transport were convinced that 14 seat vehicles (like the WHB/Waveney) had the ideal capacity in rural areas. However, many operators considered that 20-seat buses were needed to meet the emerging demands.*

Centre Right: *Mind you, in some countries, even 20-seat buses were inadequate, here we see a 28-seat WLG (truck chassis) in the Phillipines in September 1932. Note the luggage!*

Bottom Right: *Whilst 'foreign' pictures are not always popular, exports accounted for around 20% of Bedford production in the early 1930s. This WHB was operated in Malacca, Malaya.*

Top Left: *Another bus-based advertising campaign was sponsored by Eugene Permanent Wave (hair-styling), as a 'water cabaret' to travel round pleasure resorts of Britain. Led by the cross-channel swimmer Miss Sunny Lowry, the team alight from the Bedford WLB/Duple Sun Saloon outside the Barn Road House, Barnet.*

Centre Left: *Another 'team' using a Bedford/Duple demonstrator were Aston Villa Football Club, who are pictured here with the same coach seen on page 6. This view was taken at Rhyll, where the team were in training and playing golf in 1933.*

Bottom Left: *Several companies quickly built up a small fleet of Bedfords, especially in rural areas. An example was Mr. Barrett who began Barley Omnibus Co. in 1928 with a 16-seat Chevrolet. Working over unmade roads in the Pennines around Burnley and Nelson, he bought the first of these three Bedfords in 1933 (centre), and two more in 1935. By the end of 1935, each bus was averaging around 35,000 miles per year on roads as steep as 1-in-4 (25%).*

There is a question as to precisely when Plaxtons of Scarborough began their association with Bedford, and it has been written that this relationship did not begin until the introduction of the WTB chassis. However, this can now be disproved by the fact that the firm of F. W. Plaxton displayed a 20-seat WLB service bus on its stand at the Commercial Motor Show in November 1933. If anyone cares to check this statement, pictorial evidence can be found on page 379 of the December 1933 issue of the *Bedford Transport Magazine*.

However, the association with Duple was obviously the most important, and by the start of 1933 four Bedford-Duple models were being offered; the first was the WHB with a 14-seat body at £485 (£29,798) compared with the Waveney price of £470 (£28,876). Then came the 20-seat service bus at £520 (£31,948), the 20-seat coach at £550 (£33,792) and the sun saloon still at £590 (£36,249).

In all Duple bodies, the framework for the body was in prime quality ash, strengthened by special steel 'flitch' plates, connecting with 'U' channel bearers. A rear emergency door was provided, but the front doors were either of one-piece or of a folding construction depending on either a) the model being ordered, or b) the customer's own preference. Generally speaking, all the bodies on the WLB were quite similar in appearance. The service buses and Sun Saloon coaches usually had folding doors and the saloon coaches single doors. Yet that was not written in tablets of stone, nor indeed was the positioning of the door, because we know that rear and centre entrance versions were also built. The front of each bus was fitted with two windscreens, that on the driver's side being fitted with an electric wiper. Behind the door (or to the front on rear entranced models) the coach had four window bays, two of these on each side were half-drop opening but all had glass louvres at the top. The roof was also made of ash and covered with sheet steel, and the whole body was painted in two coats of primer and two coats of cellulose, which was finished in any two colours chosen by the purchaser.

Parliamentary lettering and a destination blind with six names came inclusive in the price, but full sign-writing at a cost of around £35 (£2,150) was frequently taken by the customer - often dealers would throw this in as an extra 'freebie' if it meant the difference in making the sale or not. On this point it has to be remembered that, at this time, the bus operator would normally buy his vehicle through his Vauxhall-Bedford dealer, who would normally negotiate the bodying arrangements with Duple or whoever.

Internally the Duple buses all had side panels covered in Rexine, and the roofs lined with a matching fabric. Later the Sun Saloon could be ordered with side panels covered in repp, and this became the standard finish on this luxury model by the end of 1934. Depending on the bus being bought, the roof covering would vary from repp (on the Saloon coach), to washable cream 'fabricoid' (on the service bus), or repp and even moleskin (on the Sun Saloon). The floors were all covered in lino, but the Sun Saloon had the luxury of carpeting on the gangway. The Sun Saloon, as its name implies, was basically an 'open-topped' coach, which had a mechanically operated centre section, where a canvas screen would fold or concertina back to the rear of the bus to let in both light and fresh air. In many coaches (as they got older), it was also known to let in the rain and snow as well.

Standard fittings on all the vehicles included grab and ascending door handles, chrome-plated metal fittings (e.g. ash trays, match-strikers, seat handles etc.), electric bell pushers and buzzer, licence holders, driver's mirror, life guards, first aid kit, fire extinguisher, and driver's tool kit. The seats were finished either in real leather or moquette, and the backs covered in matching repp. The Saloon Coach and the Sun Saloon also had sham curtains and full-length passenger luggage racks. The service bus was provided with eight internal circular lights fixed to the roof with chrome-plate holder, but the coaches however had eight elongated lights fastened to the window pillars. The coaches also had polished walnut garnish rails, pillar cappings and mouldings, but so too did a number of service buses and in later years this feature became standard on all three models.

Top Right: *As we have already indicated, it was not just Duple who were building on the Bedford chassis, and here we have an example of a coach built by Grose of Northampton. It seems that this firm were in fact official builders to General Motors at the time, and the plaque in the coach window confirms this.*

Centre Right: *Delivered to L. J. Ede of Par, Cornwall in 1932 this WLB is pictured alongside two OBs in the spring of 1948. All three vehicles were painted in the 'Vauxhall colours' of blue and cream, and are recorded as having bodies built by Strachans of Acton.*

Bottom Right: *Another southern operator was the firm of Bere Regis & District Motor Services, who operated a fleet of over 60 Bedfords by 1948. The oldest member of the fleet was this 1933 WLB with a Duple body, which was a regular performer on the twisting, winding route from Dorchester to Tidworth.*

The last Bedford-Duple WLB catalogue was issued in March 1935, a month after the new Bedford-Duple WTB catalogue. The final prices quoted for the complete Duple-Bedford WHBs were as follows, 20-seat Service Bus £510 (31,334), 20-seat Saloon Coach £525 (£32,256) and 20-seat Sun Saloon Coach £555 (£34,099). Comparing the two sales brochures one can see that there were obvious progressions from one Bedford model to the next, but at the same time improvements had been progressively heading towards a larger capacity vehicle. This increase in capacity would obviously help Bedford operators take on the 33-seat capacity of the bigger British bus chassis makers like AEC, Leyland and Maudslay. Yet that is not to say that large capacity Bedfords were not produced, and we know of several WHBs that were fitted with twin rear axles, giving the capability of carrying 36 to 43 seat passenger bodies.

I have not found any of these being used in Britain, but they were certainly used in Scandinavia, Australia, New Zealand and South Africa. Speaking of exports, we would mention that around 10% of WHB production went abroad, where the little Bedfords enjoyed long lives. In fact of the large number that went to South Africa, we know of one that clocked up almost half-a-million miles before its lady owner-operator decided to sell it in 1938 in order to buy a WTB.

Of those buses based on the 2-ton chassis that have lasted down to the present, we have two very remarkable early models still with us. One was a WHB with a 14-seat Waveney body, which was new to Woodhams of Melchbourne, and is shown on page 3. On its retirement in 1964, the Melchbourne Flyer was purchased by local Bedford dealers Arlington Motors, who later restored the venerable old bus. It now resides in the Vauxhall Heritage Centre at Luton, from where it ventures forth to selected promotional events, shows, and occasional starring roles in film and television. Another survivor is a modified Bedford WLG truck with a coach body by Rainforth, which can safely be regarded as the first ever Bedford bus.

This Page: *In this selection of three pictures, we see the 'Bedford Kiddies Bus'. A full report on the 36 to 38 seater Duple bodied coach was contained in the* Bedford Transport Magazine *for October 1932. A fascinating comment in the article said 'Going to school is a fairly simple matter in most families. The youngsters just run, and when school is over they run home again.' The school bus in those days was something of a rarity, and the article continued; 'One does not readily think of educational authorities as users of transport'; how things have changed in the past seven decades! However in the early 1930s a demand was emerging, especially as social responsibility for disabled and disadvantaged children was recognised. To meet this emerging demand, Bedford and Duple promoted the 'Kiddies Bus'. It was based on the WLB, but had four rows of longitudinal bench seats, arranged down the sides and centre of the coach to give maximum capacity. Mind you, the lower picture showing the bus at a zoo is a photographic fake, as the picture was taken in a school field and superimposed on another image.*

THE VYC & VXC, RURAL BUS

As stated, the demand for the larger WLB bus chassis rapidly began to outstrip that on the 14-seat WHB. Naturally, the larger capacity vehicle was a more commercial proposition, especially considering the relatively small difference in both capital acquisition and operating costs. That is not to say that there was not a demand for a small bus, it was just that this demand would have to be fulfiled with a more economical model. A few bus bodies were put on the 30-cwt WS truck chassis after its introduction in 1932, but it was the new 12-cwt VY/VX commercial chassis that offered the best potential.

Vauxhall therefore made a major decision, not only would they offer a chassis, but they would also do a 'factory-built' coach known as the Rural Bus. Initially intended as a light delivery van, the VYC had a 106 inch (2.69m) wheelbase, and was fitted with the 16.9 hp engine from the Vauxhall Cadet saloon. The VXC was given 26.33 hp power unit fitted to the W series trucks and buses. Both models had the same outward appearance, including a smart chrome pressing that surrounded the radiator grill. In essence, this created a common standard appearance through the whole range of commercial chassis.

Above: *The Bedford WS was not a common chassis for bus application, but here we see a modified 30-cwt chassis fitted out with a 'shooting brake' body and produced for work on the Estates of Earl Beatty. Note that it only has single rear wheels, as opposed to the twin rear wheels on the WHB. It also has the stronger truck type wheels, as opposed to pressed discs, and uses Firestone 32x6 truck tyres.*

Although the company had an eye to the developing future of the bus and coach industry, it clearly recognised that the biggest area of opportunity lay not in the municipal or large fleet operator, but in the small rural areas that were then being opened up. To this end an interesting article appeared on The Country Bus, in the September 1932 issue of the *Bedford Transport Magazine*. It said:-

For the benefit of any town folk who may read this article, we will explain that a rural bus is quite a car-like conveyance, made to carry about seven grown-up passengers or twelve children. The seats can be slung up to the roof, out of the way, so that when the bus isn't carrying people it can carry goods' But there were other uses too, and the article spent some time talking about the value the Rural Bus for country estates, hotels, golf clubs and schools.

The article also posed the question 'Have you ever thought what it [the Rural Bus] means to a village?' Answering rhetorically, the magazine stated 'The railway station, we will say, is a mile-and-a-half away [by no means uncommon in rural areas]. Those who want to get to it must, if there is no rural bus in the village, walk - whatever the weather, for there is never enough of them wanting to go at the same time to justify a regular bus service. The nearest town where there is any real amusement, such as a cinema, theatre or dance hall, is probably ten miles away or more. The last train for the village leaves the town hours before the amusements finish at night, and even if a late train is run for some special occasion there is still the long walk home from the station. But the rural bus will take them in and bring them home again, from door to door.'

This scenario was true up and down the land, and as the effects of the 'Depression' began to lift, and the economic situation improved, it is quite true that people wanted to travel for social activity and not just too and from work. Bus services up and down the land reflected this trend, but in the country areas new facilities were required, and light Bedford buses began to open up whole new areas. The Rural Bus was a superb concept, it could be used to take people to work early in the morning, come back and collect school children, then take the housewife to the shops. In the day it trundled around loaded with goods, and at tea time reverted to its PSV role for the homeward-bound journeys. In the evening it could be used for leisure purposes, and the VYC cost little more than a car to operate. Hotels, post offices, general stores, and even haulage contractors began operating the Rural Bus, and many new bus companies sprang up because of it.

By 1935 the VYC and VXC had been phased out in preference to the new 20hp BYC and 26hp BXC. This change was, of course heralded by the arrival of Vauxhall's new Big Six saloon car and the physical look of the car-derived commercials showed little difference from the V series that had gone before. The concept of a small 'mini-bus' remained, as we will discuss later.

Top Left: *A VYC owned by R. Finch & Son, Princetown, Devon. The bus was used to carry children from the warder's houses at Dartmoor Prison to the school in Princetown. It also catered for local football and cricket teams, the Girl Guides, Boy Scouts and the Sunday School. During the day the seats were removed and it was used to carry supplies to the prison.*

Centre Left: *The interior of a former estate bus, which once worked at a country house in the South of England, but is now operated by Francis Mahod to carry tourists around Jersey.*

Bottom Left: *Listed as an estate bus, we are unsure quite what chassis this is actually built on, and it may well be that it is yet another WS. The engine we know was the 26.33hp, and the body was built by a firm in Norfolk.*

The WTL & WTB Series

The initial success of the WHB and WLB had not been a fluke, and as the mid-1930s approached Bedford were looking to consolidate their position in the market place. The WHB had enjoyed only a brief life as demand for short chassis had rapidly declined. The WTB however went from strength to strength, but it too was finally phased out in 1935. The replacement was to be based on the new Bedford WT 3-ton truck chassis that had been introduced at the Commercial Motor Show in November 1933.

In full production by the Spring of 1934, the WT was a vehicle with semi-forward control, and a much shorter bonnet than the earlier Bedford offerings. Commercial vehicle production assumed the first call on the new model, but in December 1934 the first coach bodies were being mounted on to WT chassis, and at least two test vehicles were built. One we know to have carried a Duple Sun Saloon body, the other may well have been bodied by Plaxton's of Scarborough, but on this point the records are unclear.

Above: *One of the earlier purchasers of the WTB was the Lincolnshire firm of Enterprise & Silver Dawn. At the time they had around 80 vehicles in the fleet, including several Duple-bodied WTBs registered FW 7xxx. Here FW7279 waits at Scunthorpe with a local service beside a blackboard advertising various excursions.*

With its engine much further forward than the WHB/WLB, the new WT chassis had the centre line of its 26.3hp 6-cylinder engine directly over the front axle. Adding this factor to the long wheel base gave body-builders what they had been looking for, an economical chassis that could carry a 25- or 26-seat body. After the initial trials, on a number of 3-ton lorry chassis (we think there were eight), Duple announced it was to begin offering a 26-seat body on the WTL truck chassis at a cost of £727 (£39,134). The result was staggering and soon other firms began to follow suit, but Bedford really wanted to have builders using a specially developed bus chassis. An interesting exchange of correspondence on this matter passed between Vauxhall and Duple, Thurgood and Plaxton.

Top Left: *This publicity picture was issued in the autumn of 1936, and shows a WTB with the new 25-seat Duple Vista Observation Coach. Registered AYS 774, this coach was acquired by Scottish Airways and used on their services connecting Glasgow and the western coast of Scotland. Note the large luggage rack, which was fitted despite a larger than normal boot being built into this body by Duple.*

Centre Left: *one of the earliest WTBs to be produced, was this rear-entrance Duple bodied coach which we think later entered the fleet of Orange Coaches. Here it is seen on the 'Tilt-Test' apparatus at London Transport's Chiswick works, whilst under evaluation for Bedford in August 1935.*

Bottom Left: *Impressed by the new Bedford WTB, the Crown Purchasing Agents ordered a large batch of chassis for use as Post Buses in different countries around the Empire. Here we see a line up of six WTBs (with locally built bodies) in Gwalior, Northern India.*

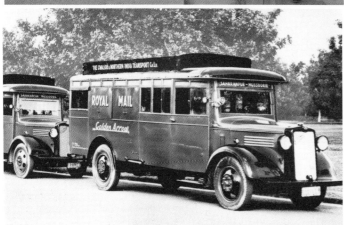

The WTB coach was formally launched at the 1935 Commercial Motor Show, with a cost price of £290 (£15,610). However, we know that several vehicles were again introduced for 'test and evaluation' before the official launch. By December 1936, Bedford were able to boast that they had produced 50 per cent of all new buses and coaches licensed during that year. This was a staggering claim considering the large number of bus chassis manufacturers in Britain at that time. Yet an examination of registration figures shows that this was no idle boast, and it seemed that bus and coach operators everywhere had been quick to appreciate both the quality and economy of the Bedford passenger range. But what was it that made the WT series so popular.

First of all it led the field in the 26-seater range, and featured a wheelbase of 167" (4.2m) and an extra long frame. Then it had a powerful 6-cylinder 3180cc, slow-revving engine rated at 26.3hp which developed 64bhp at 2,800rpm. The bore and stroke was 84.14mm x 92.25mm. Bedford advertised this as a 'long-life' engine, based on the fact that it was fitted with special compact combustion chambers that permitted a high compression ratio without detonation. It had cast-iron concave crown (dome-head) pistons, overhead valves in a detachable head and a four-bearing crankshaft. A Zenith 'down-draught' carburettor was fitted, and this incorporated an acceleration pump. Another feature was the special exhausted-heated induction manifold, and this gave better starting from cold by means of a rapid vapourisation of the mixture. A gear-type pump lubrication system, driven by an inclined shaft from the camshaft, force fed oil to the main bearing, big end bearings, and camshaft bearings.

It also lubricated the overhead valve gear, distributor drive and timing chain. At the front of the engine a 2½-gallon (11.36ltr) radiator was fitted, and this had a 4-blade fan and a chrome-plated outer shell. The entire power unit was mounted by means of a three-point fixing arrangement, which was rubber cushioned on the two front mounting points.

The transmission was through a 4-speed selective sliding gearbox, which had a mechanically operated tyre pump fitted to the near side. The latest Hardy-Spicer universal joints, complete with needle bearings, were employed, whilst the prop shaft was of the Hotchkiss open tubular type. Two prop shafts were used in tandem between the gear box and the differential, with a connecting universal joint located just below the third chassis cross member. The fully floating spiral bevel rear axle was mounted at an angle of 45 degrees to the vertical to permit greater ground clearance, a feature that also enabled shafts to be withdrawn without the need for jacking up.

The chassis was of a semi-forward control type, and the steering was a worm and wheel arrangement with a ratio of 15 to 1. Exceptional riding comfort was achieved by the generous springing, and at the front of the bus the springs were 38 inches (0.96m) long and 2¼ inches (57mm) wide and employed nine leaves. At the rear Bedford used progressive springs, which were 60 inches long (1.52m) and 2½ inches (63.5mm) wide and employed three primary and seven secondary leaves. The riding comfort was accentuated by the use of 7.50x20 tyres on 4.33x20 rims on both the front axle and the twin rear wheel axle, whilst a spare was mounted under the chassis just beyond the final cross member. A heavy-duty, large area, pressure reaction braking system, complemented the smooth riding. The vacuum-servo brakes, operated two brake shoes in each cast-iron drum (14 inch [355mm] dia. front, 16 inch [406mm] dia. rear) giving internal expansion on both the front and rear wheels, and providing a total braking area of 350 square inches. A powerful handbrake also operated the same shoes on all four wheels. A 20-gallon (90.92ltr) petrol tank was mounted on the off-side outer edge of the chassis, roughly opposite the third and fourth cross members. The 12-volt battery was located on the same side, but opposite the second cross member. The battery powered a separate Lucas starting unit and CAV constant voltage generator for the lighting systems; it also came complete with headlamps (main and dip), side lamps, combined rear and brake warning lights, speedometer and horn. The chassis came only with a scuttle, bonnet, radiator grill and front wings, but extras such as a starting handle and tool kit were included.

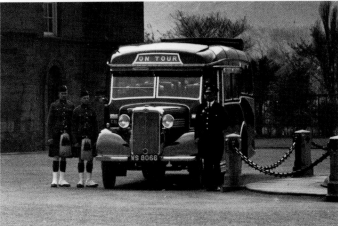

Top Right: *By the end of 1936, over 80% of all non-municipal buses in Scotland were of Bedford manufacture. This is shown by the three representative pictures on this page, commencing with this Duple bodied coach with Elliots, which worked a Pullman service on the Dumbarton, Jamestown, Loch Lomond route.*

Centre Right: *A Scottish Motor Traction WTB/Duple on tour work at Edinburgh Castle in the autumn of 1936.*

Bottom Right: *By the end of 1935 Duple offered no less than nine different bodies on the WTB chassis. Here we see a modified 'luxury coach', which was produced for evaluation purposes in 1936. This elegant coach was sent north to work with MacBraynes on the 'Royal Route' in Bonnie Scotland.*

Although numerous builders, and several bus operators built on the WTB chassis, Bedford's official partner was once again Duple who offered six standard and three special variations, of which four featured a special drop extension to the Bedford chassis frame. The models were the 20-seat or 26-seat Luxury Coach, the 20-seat or 25-seat Vista Super Luxury Coach, and the 20-seat and the 25-seat KD Super Luxury Coach (devised in conjunction with Keith Davies of Orange Coaches). The four latter models were those with the extended chassis frame. The deep side members and massive cross members that Bedford had used on the chassis were immediately appreciated by Duple, and they were able to apply a slightly heavier construction than that used on earlier Bedford chassis.

The range started with the Luxury Coach where the 20-seat cost £735 (£39,565) and the 26-seat cost £750 (£40,372) , which was designed basically as a rear entrance coach, but could be obtained with a front sliding door by special order at no extra cost. The 20 seater had four double seats each side, and a four-seat bench across the rear. The spacing between the double seats was 33 inches (0.83m) on the offside, and 36 inches (0.91m) on the near side. The 26-seater was more cramped, and it had a five-seat rear bench, with a three-seat bench in front of it on the offside, Four double seats were also located on the off-side, each with a spacing of 30^1/2 inches (0.77m).

The nearside of the coach had five double seats, with a spacing of just 29 inches (0.73m), despite the fact that the front set of seats was almost parallel with the driver's seat. A driver's/emergency door was located at the front offside of the body. The framework on which the individually-fitted steel panels were fixed, was constructed from well-seasoned ash, which was hand selected from the timber yard of J. Glikstein & Son, Stratford, London E15. Steel strengthening plates were employed at strategic locations, and two of the side pillars on each side were steel-capped. The roof was also constructed from ash, and a sliding 'sunshine panel' by Sunsaloon Bodies of Birmingham was fitted before the domed section at the rear.

As can be seen from the picture above, the front of the roof had a destination blind, and a steel sun visor protruded out over the chrome edged windscreen. The screen itself was produced by Elliott's of Hendon and was divided by a central pillar; on the driver's side the screen was split in two. The larger lower portion was a top-hinged opening panel, on which was mounted the single electric windscreen wiper motor and blade. The side windows were to Widney Stuart patents, and two 'Simplastic' special frameless full drop windows were fitted on each side. Air was circulated through the body by means of special roof-mounted vents and ventilators on the scuttle. Window ventilators were provided by chrome-trimmed louvres above the four main side windows.

16

Top Left: *Externally all Bedford-Duple coaches, like this KD for Orange Coaches would be prepared, filled, and rubbed and painted with cellulose supplied by Glasso Paint Products of Perrivale, Middlesex, which was applied in up to two colours. Parliamentary lettering (showing the operators name and address) and six blind destinations were applied free, but other sign-writing came as an extra charge. A spacious rear luggage compartment and a spare-wheel access panel were provided at the rear, but a few coaches (like BMP 420) featured a novel side-stowage area, which came with or without a covering body panel - but such an arrangement was not long-lasted.*

Top Right and Below: *Whilst the KD may have been the luxury offering from Duple, there was an even more elegant coach by Mulliner's of Northampton. Makers of high class limousine car bodies, Mulliner's were to apply their standards of quality production to this WTB bodied for the Liss & District Omnibus Company, and they also achieved a semi-forward control to provide extra leg room between the seats.*

ARTHUR MULLINER LTD. NORTHAMPTON

ARTHUR MULLINER LTD. NORTHAMPTON

Internally, the bus had quite an elegant feel to it, and this is shown to good effect in the official Bedford-Duple publicity photograph seen opposite. Pictures of bus and coach interiors are not that well featured in bus books, but this was such a superb picture we felt that it required the justice of an entire page in order to accompany the details that follow. At the front of the coach quilted or carpet type engine cowl covers were available at an extra cost to 'disguise' the bleak looking front end, which really did look out of place against the polished walnut rails, window fillets and cappings. Roof panels were produced by ICI (Rexine) from Hyde in Cheshire, and offered a scratch-proof, durable, damp resistant, easily-cleaned and hygienic finish that was 'artistic in appearance'. The floor had a linoleum covering in the seating area using a colour which matched the upholstery, whilst a rubber mat was used down the central isle.

The seat cushions were made from Dunlopillo, which was then advertised as 'Life's Latest Luxury'. Coverings came in an uncut Yorkshire moquette, which was supplied either by Holdsworths of Halifax or Firths from Heckmondwike. The seat backs and side panels were made from repp from Holdsworths or Firths, using a design that harmonised with the moquette. Leather was used to trim the seats. Internal lighting was supplied by seven lights, normally from a firm called BMAC of Holloway N7, who also supplied the 8-day electric clock. The fire extinguisher, first aid kit and licence holder came from Romac of Hendon, whilst Wilfred Overton of Walsall supplied items like seat back pulls, ash trays, seat numbers and the 'allway' adjustable driver's seat. For an optional extra of 19 guineas (£1,076) you could have the Philco Model 902TC 2-band coach radio supplied by Delco-Remmy & Hyatt. Window curtains and a driver's night time screen completed the internal specification

The Vista Super Luxury Coach came out at £815 (£43,871) for the 20-seat and £825 (£44,409) for the 26-seat, and was well worth the extra cost. Whilst not dissimilar to the Luxury Coach, the Super Luxury coach had a much more streamlined feel to it. The passenger door was now at the front, and the saloon had two large window bays each side, separated by a central body pillar. The window bay was divided into two halves, and the window panels either side of the central pillar were drop-opening panes. The driver's/emergency door and the passenger door each had a square shaped glass pane, and ahead of these a small quarter light window angled slightly towards the windscreen. A modest amount of stainless steel trim (chrome on some vehicles) was a welcome feature. The large sweeping side flash on the Luxury coach was replaced by a much more discrete side flash and special streamlining round the rear mudguard that swept down to the rear of the bus. A much larger luggage compartment was fitted, and this extended under the rear seats.

Internally the specification was similar to the Luxury coach, but the seats rose slightly towards the rear of the vehicle. On the 20-seat model there were four double seats each side, with 35 inch (0.89m) spacing on the nearside, and 33 inch (0.83m) spacing on the offside. A luxurious rear seat provided four comfortable berths, and an armrest located in the centre gave a 2x2 seating arrangement.

The 25-seat version had a single bench-type seat giving five places, and five double seats were provided either side with $29^{1}/_{2}$ inch (0.75m) between them. Ventilation was by special dash ventilators and chrome-plated V louvres over the side windows. An ascending handle was also fitted to the door, making access easier. The roof could also be had with a domed back and sun-saloon head, or with a half-sliding panel roof. The seven roof lights on the Luxury Coach were now supplanted by eight pillar lights, but it employed the same full length parcel racks.

The third option, the KD Super Luxury Coach cost the same as the Super Luxury Coach, coming in at £815 (£43,871) for the 20-seat and £825 (£44,409) for the 26-seat. Many of the fittings were as previously given, but from the outside the difference in the coaches was visibly noticeable . Behind the passenger and emergency doors, the KD had four separate window panels, of which the rear two panels were at a higher level. The rear window was shaped to the downward sweep of the body at the back, and roughly two-thirds the size of the others. Five of the windows were drop-opening.

The seats were to the same configuration as the Super Luxury Coach, but the rear two sets of double seats and the rear bench were positioned higher than the others. A fully opening sunroof by Wilfred Overton was fitted, and this allowed the roof panel to be slid from the front of the bus right to the back, where it would concertina down just above and behind the rear seat. The bus could also be ordered with a standard sun roof and a domed back. A few variations of the KD were even built with a full front, making a stylish luxury 'observation coach', which is shown in the *Duple Annual 1937*.

In many ways this KD was a cross with the Luxury Coach, but its sides had quite prominent streamlining, a feature which had become in vogue due to the streamlining of the crack express locomotives of the day. Both wheels had a curved streamline feature sweeping up the leading edge, then sweeping down to a vanishing point. The rear streamline ended at the back of the coach, but the one curving round the front wheel, reached its vanishing point just before the rear wheel arch. The rear windows of this luxury observation coach were stepped slightly higher than the Luxury Coach, but not as high as the KD, although the rear seats were at the same elevation as those on the KD. A slight triple-tailed side flash ran below the two rear windows, disguising the difference in height with the lower windows. A domed roof was fitted, and three long roof-lights were fitted with an opaque glass to give added illumination within the saloon. Vauxhall records show that only about 40 of these 26-seat coaches were built, and at £975 (£52,484) is it surprising? However, this extra cost did provide an attendants' seat alongside the driver, and 'a combined radio and courier announcement system'.

The final variant offered by Duple was the Service Bus, which could be found as either a rear or front entry model, and with either sliding doors, folding doors, or in a few cases without doors at all. There was a certain 'family' similarity in the Duple Service Bus bodies, but there were many variations on the theme, and as a result no published price list was issued until 1938.

Top Left: *Another firm regularly building on the WTB chassis in the mid-1930s were W. L. Thurgood of Ware. This 26-seater WTB features the new Willenhall bonnet and radiator pressings that would become familiar on the O type, whilst the coach itself has the new 'Easiway' roof opening system.*

Centre Left: *Although prices for the Bedford-Duple Service Bus variant were initially quoted 'on application', by the start of 1938 a list price of £710 (£38,219) was announced for the 20-seater, with the 26-seater costing just £10 (£538) more. Here a batch of 1938 service buses for Western Welsh are captured on WTB chassis outside the Duple works.*

Bottom Left: *Described in the files as an 'advanced coach chassis', this may be one of the two prototype OBs produced at the end of 1938. According to the information on the back of the picture, the body builder is recorded as F.W. Plaxton!*

For the summer of 1938 Bedford announced it was to update the WTB chassis, and the most notable development was the improvement of the 64 bhp engine. The modified engine had a cubic capacity of 27.34cc and developed 28hp/72bhp, giving substantially more power for what was then (but as yet un-announced) an impending plan to introduce a chassis capable of carrying a 29-seat body. The new chassis would become the famous OB, which was officially introduced in July 1939. However, once again, Bedford had an OB chassis ready much earlier, and a dealer brochure published in November 1938 carries a picture of this. This picture is shown on page 24 and may have been taken as early as June 1938.

To the bus operator, the immediate changes were in the improved WTB and the most noticeable of these was the re-styled front end. In advance of the new O-Type being introduced, the bonnet panels and radiator grill (fabricated by Willenhall Motor & Radiator Company) for this model were fitted to the WTB. This has often caused mistakes in the identity between late WTBs and early OBs.

The progression from the WTB to the OB was in fact quite subtle, and it is clear that Vauxhall had decided that introducing an entirely new vehicle on to the bus market in an unproven form would be detrimental to their position as leaders in the small bus field. Indeed, when the last of the 2,320 WTB chassis rolled off the Luton assembly line, the Bedford Marque accounted for a staggering 70% off all new buses and coaches in the non-municipal market. This had been achieved inside just eight years, and it took the company into a prominent position in supplying what Britain would need during the dark days of World War II that lay ahead. In June 1938 Vauxhall prepared a document for the Government to show what capacity and facilities it had available, the photograph album that was produced to accompany that report also makes a fascinating compilation of the Luton Works just prior to the conflict. It was almost as though the O series had been built in readiness for the coming war, and perhaps it had, but in the years that followed it really proved its metal.

THE K AND M TYPE

As the 1930s drew to a conclusion, Vauxhall had firmly established themselves in the commercial vehicle market, offering vehicles in the 7-cwt to 3-ton range. The sales were beyond expectations, but there was a need to move onward and upward. The mechanical side of the range was progressing steadily, but by the mid-1930s the Bedford trucks and buses had a 'dated' feel about their outward appearance.

As early as 1936 it had been decided to produce a distinctive look for the Bedford range, and this was probably due to a desire to get away from the Chevrolet-look of the earlier models. No doubt this led to the discussions between Luton management and the Willenhall Motor & Radiator Company early in 1938, who were soon receiving orders to produce a new range of pressings to form cab, roof, front scuttle, doors, bonnets and radiators for a new range of Bedford trucks.

Above: *This is a post-war K-Type with a Spurling body, and used for the National Blood Transfusion Service as a nurses bus. However, just to show how the language has changed in the past half century, I can tell you this picture was originally captioned as a 'Spurmobus with a bleeding team on the way to a blood-getting session.'*

The result of this styling change was the attractive rounded appearance of the new K, M, and O Types, which came out in the summer of 1939. As is well known, the advent of World War II put paid to any real commercial progress with this range of vehicles, but they were used extensively for military application throughout the period 1939-45. The K-Type replaced the WS, and was referred to as a 30- to 40-cwt model on a 120 inch - (3.048m) chassis, but after the war it was just described as a 30-cwt model. The M-Type was a 2/3-ton chassis, available in long (143 inch - 3.632m) or short (120 inch - 3.048m) wheelbase.

Early models retained the quaint pressed steel disc wheels of the VY and WS commercials. Tyres were 6x20 all round on all models, except when the K-Type had single rear wheels, when 32x6 ware used. The brakes were 13 inch (330mm) internal diameter at the front, and 14 inch (355.6mm) at the rear. On the M-Type a Clayton Dewandre Vacuum Servo Unit was installed as standard. However, it was noted that heavy application of the brakes would result in locking of the wheels and heavy tyre wear.

The overall length of the K-Type was 196$\frac{1}{4}$ inches (4.98m), whilst the SWB M-Type was fractionally longer at 196$\frac{1}{2}$ inches (4.99m) and the LWB model was 219$\frac{1}{4}$ inches (5.57m). The K-Type was 70$\frac{1}{2}$ inches (1.79m) wide, slightly less than the M-Type at 77 inches (1.96m). The chassis was powered by the new 27.34hp engine, and the specifications for this are shown elsewhere in this book. The history of K and M models is quite interesting, but it does not have that big a bearing on the Bedford bus story, and the numbers bodied for this type of application were considerably less than they had been with the Rural Bus. Some may say that low capacity buses have no place in this book at all, but the K and M were another import bench mark in the Bedford story and can not be omitted.

Top Left: *A 1939 SWB M-Type with a Mulliner body, produced for the Mostyn & Kennilworth Hotels, and used as a 'station bus', for staff transport and also for touring.*

Centre Left: *The body builder is not recorded on this 40cwt K-Type which is fitted with an unusual back axle arrangement, featuring twin rear wheels using pierced 3.75x20 rims and 7.5x20 Firestone tyres. It is obviously an export model, and it may have been one of a batch ordered by the Great Western Railway of Brazil in 1945.*

Bottom Left: *This is the 30-cwt K-Type, with the Spurling Spurmobus 15-seat body. As the bus still retains the pressed disc wheel rims, it seems likely that this is an early production. It was used by the Ministry of Food Production, and may therefore be a wartime model.*

Top Right: *Here we see a 1939 M-Type maximum capacity school bus designed to carry 40 children. A similar body was used to form the basis of prison vans, and five of these were allocated to the London area in October 1939.*

Bottom Right: *For operators of today who are plagued with ripped moquette, graffiti and stained carpets, the interior of the maximum capacity school bus must be absolutely wonderful. Good solid surfaces, robust wooden benches, easily wiped-down surfaces, and a 'cattle-truck' seating philosophy, are all clearly seen in this 1939 view. As a father of four, grandfather of three, educator and occasional bus driver, what more can I say?*

THE PRE-WAR OB

Just before the outbreak of World War II, Bedford launched its new bus chassis, the OB (seen inset). Many commentators have expressed a view that its timing was unfortunate in view of the events soon to unfold, but it was quite to the contrary, as Vauxhall were well aware of what was to come. Therefore the introduction of its K, M and O models came about **because** of the expected upturn in demand for economically produced commercial chassis. Indeed, booklets were produced for the Government in 1938, showing the capacity of the works, and the versatility of the products it made. One of these products was the 'new' OB bus to be released in 1939.

However, by the time the coach was released, large 'blocks' of Vauxhall's production had been reserved for military vehicles and the fact that the new OB did not make immediate 'in-roads' into the British bus market should be no surprise. Other writers have commented upon the fact that Vauxhall did little to publicise the new coach, but again this was not an issue that concerned the company in 1939. Simply put, they had more than enough work to keep them fully occupied, and they also knew that the OB had a secure future. For this reason, I do not propose to go into too much detail on the pre-war OB, save to say that very few chassis were produced between July and September 1939, and that the bus would emerge in its wartime variant as soon as the immediate need for trucks had been satisfied.

Above:

This immaculate 27-hp Bedford WS with a 13-seat Churchill body (which is also seen on the front cover) is owned and operated by Francis Mahood of St. Saviours in Jersey. It was built in 1937 and began work on a country estate in the South of England, undertaking the type of function that many WS types were used for and thus earned for them the name Country Bus. Elsewhere in the book we show a picture of a 13-seater bus running a service from Dartmoor Prison, and this vehicle once undertook a similar role, for after its days on the estate it was used at Pentonville Prison. From there it moved to Surrey where it was purchased for restoration by Francis. With its attractive colour scheme, the bus is still in regular use carrying visitors round museum sites in Jersey along with two Duple-bodied Bedford OBs of 1949 and 1950 vintage.

Above: *To prove the longevity of Bedford coaches we show this picture of a Duple bodied WTB, which is seen enjoying a second lease of life operating a heritage coach tour service from the Channel Island Ferry car park to Upwey. Advertised as the 'Comfy Coach' in the 1930-s, this stylish body was built at the Hendon Works in North London. The style lines on the coach side were part of the 1930s vogue of streamlining, due to the popularity of the express locomotives of the day, which the coach operators tried to imitate in their own way. Note the addition of modern indicators below the bumper, which have been fitted for safety reasons.*

Left: *This is the wartime bus offering from Bedford, the OWB, which is seen here in the two-tone green/beige livery of Eagle Coachways of Tench in Shropshire, and operating the service from Wellington to Trench. Such a sight would have been familiar all over Britain right into the 1950s.*

Above: *In this series of books, you will find that we have a bit of a passion for buses in the Shetland Islands - because Trans-Pennine are sponsoring the restoration of two Bedford coaches from these islands. On this page we show a pair of Bedford O types that operated with Irvine Bros. of Boddam at the southern end of the most northerly islands in Britain. In the upper picture we have a 1950 Mulliner-bodied OB in the company's red and cream livery. Carrying a Shetland registration plate (PS 1977) the bus spent its entire working life in the Shetlands.*

Below: *We see an SMT-bodied OB, which was new to Scottish Omnibuses as fleet number C187. For those who are interested in buses on this of group islands, Trans-Pennine are to publish a book* Shetland Island Buses in the 20th Century *at the end of December 2000. So at this stage we aren't giving away too much about these buses!* Both Gordon Jamieson

Above:

Whilst talking of the north of Scotland, here we have a Bedford OB (chassis number 131963) of 1950 vintage, offering luxury travel from Lands End to John O' Groats
Yet despite what it says on the cant rail panels, it is doubtful whether the vehicle ever actually operated a service between these destinations.
The bus does, however carry a Dundee registration plate.
Seen here in the livery of McNeil's of Todmorden (West Yorkshire), the bus once had its moment of glory, and whilst in McNeil's ownership it was re-painted yellow and green and used in a television advertisement which, if I recall correctly, was made for the British Petroleum Company.

THE UBIQUITOUS OWB

If ever any one vehicle changed the face of modern bus and coach operation, then this vehicle has to be the Bedford OB bus chassis. Its introduction in 1939, along with other vehicles in Bedford's K, M, and O series was a deliberate advancement brought about ahead of the coming conflict, and was not a range of vehicles stunted by the onset of war. The three vehicle ranges were a defined improvement on what had gone before, and were a direct response from Vauxhall to the British government's request for 20,000 light to medium trucks if war should break out.

There can be no doubt that the O Type was in the planning from 1937 onwards, and the first experimental models appeared in the summer of 1938. Naturally this development was a closely guarded secret, partially for commercial reasons and partially for reasons of national secrecy. Quite when the O prototypes were built remains a matter of debate, and for whatever reason the records are not clear. However, two things we do know; one is that an O-Type lorry was received by the Royal Engineers in December 1938, and two is the fact that the OB chassis was photographed in June 1938 for use in a new bus brochure that the company were then designing.

As we stated earlier, the pre-war life of the OB bus did not exactly set the world alight, and apart from a 'dealer's brochure' printed in February 1939, there seems to have been very little in the way of pre-war publicity. It is clear that, had Neville Chamberlain's peace-pact gone ahead with Germany, business would have been as normal and the OB would have enjoyed a major launch in the various commercial vehicle shows at the end of 1939. But by May 1939, Vauxhall had begun to gear up for the war effort that would see over a quarter of a million commercial vehicles and 5,000 tanks being made in the next six years. Bearing in mind that the Bedford coach was aimed mainly at the small operator running a mixture of service and excursion work, there was a reluctance at promoting the new bus into an area that would witness severe curtailment if war broke out.

The Government were more interested in commercial vehicles to meet the needs of the armed forces, but the bus was not ignored and discussions about maximum capacity buses (30+ seaters to carry service personnel) were still ongoing when war was finally declared in September. Plans were in place for military and essential PSV buses on the OB chassis, to the drawing above (originated in January 1940) but it was decreed that in the meantime trucks fitted with bench seats would meet the immediate military requirements.

Top Left: *Only here for the beer? This fleet of OWBs was used by Tadcaster brewers John Smith to transport staff from nearby towns.*

Centre Left: *According to Vauxhall's publicity material on the OWB, 'This 'economy-type' bus has been built to comply with wartime specification issued by the Ministry of Supply. There are no 'frills' or individual body styles, but the coach is durable, workman-like and serviceable, and all 32 seats are arranged to face forward. Reliability, performance and long life are assured by the Bedford (special) 174in wheelbase coach chassis.' This example (FDE 691), complete with lady driver, was owned by Green Motors Ltd.*

Bottom Left: *Not all OWBs were painted brown or grey during the war years, for example a batch of OWBs acquired by Southern National in 1943 were painted in an attractive green and cream scheme. Here DOD 560 crosses a watersplash in North Cornwall on 23rd May 1943.*

With regard to new vehicles for public transport services, there was (strangely enough) a reduction in the initial demand. This came about due to a severe curtailment of almost all excursion work and a general reduction in many public services, and in December 1939 the Ministry of Supply told Vauxhall that there was a national surplus of around 280 buses in the 2- to 3-ton capacity range. Accordingly they insisted no further production capacity be allocated to bus chassis production, and as a consequence the OB bus all but disappeared. Large parts of Vauxhall's capacity were taken up with non-vehicle production, and many skilled workers were enlisted into the armed forces. In their stead came callow youths, old men brought out of retirement, and an army of women workers. The recruitment of women to work at Luton was in no means unusual, for similar arrangements were being implemented at factories and munitions works all around Britain. This, however, was to have its own impact on the demand for a re-emergence of bus chassis production.

By 1941 the Ministry of Supply were forced to concede that there were now no longer enough buses to meet the demands, and it agreed to allow several manufacturers to complete those vehicles that had been in production when the embargo had been placed in 1939. But in effect it only 'un-froze' parts that had been held in stock for over two years, and allowed these to be completed, although it did not sanction any new building. As the Ministry of Supply had strict control over all rubber, steel and timber supplies at this time, it is easy to see how control was achieved. Yet, the demand for buses continued to grow because the existing vehicles were ageing rapidly due to their extended workloads and reduced maintenance, and at the same time substantial numbers were being lost due to enemy bombing. Therefore it was decided that three types of 'Utility' bus would be provided, namely a double-decker, a half cab single-decker and a lightweight service bus. The double-decker and the half cab were to be built on a number of different chassis, but as for the lightweight bus, Bedford was given the sole licence to supply.

Designated the OWB (wartime OB), the new bus was to use the 1939 OB chassis and a Duple-designed body, although the building of this would be shared by Duple, SMT of Glasgow, Charles Roe of Leeds, and (later on) Mulliner of Birmingham. However, a small number were built by other coachbuilders, an example being ERM 533 new to Hartness of Penrith with a body by Cressbank.

There was no pretence at any luxury, and seating capacity was increased to 32, drawing on a design for RAF buses that was put forward in 1939 but never implemented. Closer spacing of the seats, all of which were hardwood slats on metal frames, achieved this increased capacity but did so at the expense of passenger comfort.

Framework for the OWB initially employed oak and teak, but the MoS then released a quantity of American hardwood that had originally been purchased for furniture production. However, supplies of good quality timber eventually became exhausted and unseasoned ash and pitch pine were employed in less-essential areas like longitudinal rails. Joints were re-enforced with mild steel bracing plates, and steel ties were used on the roof-sticks. Externally the OWB had a skin of 20swg steel, and the joints covered with a steel beading strip. The OWB retained the rounded radiator grill, and bonnet of the pre-war OB, and thus avoided the squared off angular appearance of Bedford's wartime trucks. A certain degree of angularity was to be noted in the roof panels, as this obviated the need to fit the expensive beaten curved panels used on the front and rear of pre-war models.

Two permanent louvre air-intake grills were fitted on the front roof panel, and generally one half-drop opening window was fitted to each side of the OWB. The screen on the driver's side was a two-part affair, the lower section being a top-hinged opening panel. The top section was designed to carry glass, but in the interests of economy was often blanked out with sheet steel. In later years some operators replaced this with glass. Glazing in all windows was ordinary 32oz sheet glass, except for the windscreen and the internal partition behind the driver, which had the luxury of safety glass.

Doors were usually at the front, and to a 'jack-knife' pattern, but some were made with rear doors and an open platform for the Royal Navy and sent to Bermuda. An emergency door was provided at the rear of the bus, and situated in the centre of the back panel at the end of the centre gangway. Almost all OWBs were given a standard brown paint scheme, regardless of the operator's usual livery, and the wing edges were picked out in white paint due to the blackout regulations. The buses retained two headlamps, unlike other vehicles (which were reduced to a single lamp), but the size of the headlamps was substantially reduced from the size of the pre-war OBs.

Right: *The firm of Bond Brothers linked the coal-mining villages of Willington, Oakenshaw, Sunnybrow and Hunwick, with Bishop Auckland. I travelled many miles on their buses whilst I was a student at Durham University, and they are still active today. Yet their place in bus history was assured by their receipt of the 1,000th OWB, registered JTN 915. These are just three of the pictures of what has to be the most photographed Bedford bus in World War II!*

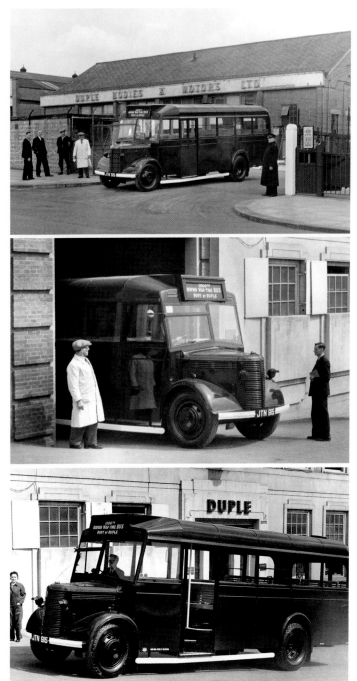

Top Left: *We now see a trio of post-war OWBs, beginning with Duple-bodied GXD 642. It was being used by Bere Regis & District Transport in March 1948, when photographed in Trinity Street Dorchester heading for Broadmayne.*

Centre Left: *This Duple-bodied OWB was modified in 1946 by Pearsons of Liverpool, and fitted with more comfortable seating to carry 29 passengers. The rear of the bus was also modified, and the exit door relocated in order to provide a bench seat.*

Bottom Left: *Several OWBs were re-bodied for the Ministry of Transport & Civil Aviation, one example being this Mulliner-bodied 30-seater (HYL 144) seen at London Airport in August 1955.*

Top Right: *And finally, a real post-war mixture of OBs and OWBs in the Exeter garage of Greenslades.*

Internally the buses were devoid of any luxury, as evidenced by the wooden seats. The tongue and groove pine floor panels were covered with linoleum, which extended up the sides of the bus as far as the seat rails. Side panels were notable by their absence, and internally they were usually painted up to the window rail, and then coated in stain above this. The cost was £800 (£28,128) complete, but buyers had to obtain a 'Licence To Acquire' from the Ministry of War Transport before an order would be accepted.

The OWB became an instantly popular bus, and not only with small operators (like the majority of pre-war Bedfords), but also with larger fleets and municipal operators as well. Yet there were several problems, notably with severe reduction in the lift of overhead exhaust valves that became evident when the buses had achieved a few thousand miles in service. The problem was more related to the poor quality of low-octane fuel then available, rather than any major defect in the engine. But it was a serious problem nevertheless, and all dealers were sent a modification sheet detailing improvement that had to be made to the tappets, valves and guides, along with a 5° advance in the ignition timing. Another problem was that of cornering and poor road holding, which was eventually put down to the full load on the chassis and the use of 5.50x20 tyres fitted on all six wheels. This was soon changed to 8.25x20 tyres all round, and then back to 7.50x20 front and 8.25x20 rear tyres by the end of 1944. In the summer of that year the 1,000th Duple OWB was turned out.

Yet, as we have shown it was not just Duple that were bodying the OWB at this time, and when Duple produced the 1,000th OWB body, their co-producers Roe and SMT had built a further 800 bodies between them. Roe eventually relinquished its interest, as it was forced to concentrate on double-deck bodies. By this time Roe's force of female workers were considered adept enough to tackle the bigger jobs that had been curtailed when the men went off to the armed forces. One of those who left Roe was my late-father-in-law, who had left the comparative warmth of the Leeds workshops for the bitter cold of a corvette patrolling the North Atlantic.

It has been written that there was no 'relaxation' of the Utility specification on the OWB, although it is clear that improvements began to take place both before and after the cessation of hostilities. In many cases these improvements were mostly cosmetic enhancements to provide greater passenger comfort. Several builders offered curved roof domes to replace the angular front and rear roof panels of the early OWBs, although this feature had officially been relaxed by the MoS in 1944. After the war, the 32-seat capacity was considered too great for the chassis size, and 'Construction & Use' regulations demanded a reduction to 28 seats.

I have long had doubts on what had been previously written on the subject of 'relaxation' on the OWB, then I came across a letter to all Bedford Distributors and Dealers.written by Vauxhall's Director of Sales, Mr. A. F. Palmer Phillips on 14th February 1945. It read:-

We are pleased to inform you that as a result of representation made by the coach operators to the Ministry of Supply, we have been instructed to incorporate a few improvements in the bodywork of the Bedford Wartime Utility Bus. The improvements are:-1) The existing wooden seats are replaced with upholstered seats, including spring cushions and padded squabs trimmed in standard brown leather, the seat backs being trimmed in a harmonising brown repp.

The seating accommodation is unaltered. 2) Two additional half-drop windows will be fitted, making four in all. 3) Glass interior lampshades will replace the ARP type now in use. 4) A greater volume of lighting is made available for the front indicator board.

The price of the body will be increased to £460, the chassis price remaining at £413, the price of the complete Bus becoming £873. The handling allowance on the body will be 5% as before. These changes will become effective on all deliveries made from Messrs. Duple Bodies and Motors Ltd. on and after April 3rd 1945. We are enclosing a list of your customers whose buses will include the new improvements and it will be necessary for you to contact these customers at once and get the original order amended to the new price. It should be noted too that all orders booked from now on must be at the increased price as no buses will be available with the Wood Slatted seats after April 2nd.

This became effective at the start of April, and stayed the standard specification for the OWB until the model was phased out after OB production resumed in October 1945. Several of the latter OWBs were bodied by Duple with their MkII Service Bus body. In all 348 OWBs were produced for military use in this period, but far greater in number were the 2,842 that entered public service.

POST-WAR EXPORTS AND THE ALMET

Before returning to the re-introduction of OB, we must consider the situation that faced Vauxhall in the immediate post-war period. At this time the Government were insisting on a massive export quota from British vehicle manufacturers in order to help gain foreign income and thus pay off the crippling war debts that the country faced. The scope of this export drive was phenomenal, and whilst we know some readers do not like to see 'foreign-looking' buses in books like this, the export market is inescapable. Indeed so substantial was this business, that one of the early orders (placed in October 1945) was for a batch of 229 OBs for Ceylon. Most were supplied merely as chassis, but 12, including the two buses pictured opposite were sent complete with Duple bodies. Within 12 months of the war ending, 10,000 Bedfords had been exported. Although the majority were truck chassis, a fair number were OWB/OB chassis.

Large numbers were supplied to European countries who were rebuilding after the ravages of war, and Holland was a particularly avid buyer of the OB. In tropical markets a massive demand emerged, and to meet this a new development sprang from the basic design of the OWB, and proved to be an exceptionally useful model for both Bedford and Duple. This was the Almet bus, which basically meant all-metal construction. It came into being late in 1945, and its origins are directly based on the wartime experiences of both Bedford and Duple.

Yet surprisingly little has been written about a model that played a significant role in the way that all buses and coaches would soon be made. It is also worth noting, that at a time when the British Government were exporting vehicle manufacturers to 'export or die', the Almet took British buses into markets that had been hitherto denied to them because wooden-framed buses were unsuitable for the climate.

Top Left: *From the picture shown left we can see just how close the first Almet design was to the OWB and there is a good reason for this. In truth the image you see above is not a photograph, but a composite image made from parts of OWB photos and drawings, re-touching with china clay or ink. The front end of the bus, including radiator, bonnet and windscreen are all real, as are the wheels. The beading, door and parts of the roof are all cut from original photographs of an OWB, but the rest of it is purely an artist's work.*

Top and Bottom Right: *This pair of images shows the first of two complete Bedford-Duple OWBs being loaded for export. These vehicles were part of a large order destined for Ceylon (now Sri Lanka), and feature modified versions of the utility body.*

The Almet was a series that has been described as 'a confusing collection of different designs'. But was this the case? Outwardly one has to admit that there were a plethora of different looking buses in the Almet series, but in reality there was just one major design. In fact it was a design that could be adapted to meet the different needs of operators, and the different needs of countries or continents come to that. What is more, not all Almets were exported, and several saw service in this country. Perhaps it is the concept that this was purely a foreign bus that has kept it out of bus books in the past, but the all-metal bus was such an important step in the public service vehicle, it deserves far greater coverage.

I may well get taken to task for showing too many pictures of export buses in this book, but I rest on the importance of the concept to sustain my decision. Builders had tried all-metal bodies in Britain as far back as the early-1930s, and Duple built their first all-metal body in late-1933. They produced several more in 1934, and it is clear that they would have expanded into the concept of steel-framing with aluminium panelling had war not intervened. In reality Duple were keeping a watchful eye on Britain's railways, where wooden-framed coaches had been shown to be substantially more liable to impact damage when compared with the new metal-framed carriages. For those readers who want to know more about these safety issues, I would refer them to my series of books *Trains In Trouble*.

Bearing in mind the Ministry of Transport were the regulators of both the railways and the bus and coach industry, it is not surprising that change from one field of transport spread into others. Quietly at first, but essentially increasing in pressure, the Ministry sought to advance safety in any type of vehicle body in which passengers were carried. True, there was not the hue and cry in coach safety that attended the railways, but it was coming. Indeed, had it not been for World War II, I am convinced that all-metal bodies would have been insisted upon in passenger vehicles far sooner than they would eventually evolve. But in the absence of enforced regulations, the official desire for progress was tempered by the commercial fact that all-steel bodies had (thus far) not been proved in the bus and coach industry, added to which were the high costs of staff re-training and equipment conversion.

Top Left: *This picture has been shown in another publication and described as a wooden-framed body for Nigeria, but writing on the rear of the print indicates that it had a composite body. Namely a wooden front, with an Almet body to the rear and looks very similar to the drawing shown previously. It had 38 longitudinal seats.*

Centre Left: *The interior of another composite body, this time a left-hand drive model for Europe.*

Bottom Left: *Mounted only on the Bedford OB chassis, the Almet was sold with a world-wide service back-up, which in turn was provided by the international dealer service organisation of Vauxhall, Bedford or General Motors. This trio of Almets were part of a batch of 30 buses supplied to the East African Railways in July 1949. The vehicles feature 1st class seats covered in Christie Tyler fabric, but only wooden slatted seats for 2nd class travellers. It also had steel panel shutters in lieu of window glass, and a letter box on the nearside for mail collection.*

For the manufacturers there were added advantages in the construction of all-metal bodies, namely in the field of pre-fabrication, as panels, roof-sections etc, could all be produced on sub-assembly lines and put on to the chassis at a later stage.

In the export market this offered the opportunity to supply buses in kit form, known as CKD (completely knocked-down). Indeed, there was the distinctive advantage of being able to send a body and chassis separately to the point of destination, and until it was assembled these two essential components need never ever come together. In fact this happened only rarely, as Bedford chassis were sent to Hendon, and then put together with a CKD kit and exported. But the potential was there, and the concept was good.

It also had another advantage, for in the case of severe damage, it was quite simple to ship out another panel to the user, who would simply remove a damaged unit and bolt a new one into place. This had obvious appeal in those countries where body-building facilities were limited. The Almet therefore had an immediate appeal to two official bodies, both of whom were concerned with export buses. The first was the Crown Purchasing Agents who purchased supplies for countries within the British Empire, or those lands protected by it. The second was the Ministry of Supply, Foreign Vehicle Section, who controlled the exports of trucks and buses and thus helped bring in much-needed foreign cash to assist Britain's balance of payments problem.

This is what Duple's own brochure had to say about the bus that it had designed for the roads of the world. 'Many years of experience in the supply of buses to users in all parts of the world have gone into the design of the new Duple Almet Bedford Bus. It represents an entirely new advance in bus design - a bus specially engineered, styled and fitted out to meet the requirements of overseas users and available in a special pack so that it can be shipped economically and assembled speedily at destination.....'

The basic idea behind the Almet bus was derived from Duple's experience during the war when they built assemblies for heavy bombers in addition to essential bus construction. In peace-time they decided to use six major assemblies to make up a simple, sturdy and robust export model. No timber was used in the construction and extreme precautions were taken against rust, including special grades of paint, hence it was ideal for tropical and humid conditions. The design was such that final assembly could be carried out without expensive tools and no welding or soldering was required.

The base of the Almet was a three-part floor section, which was radically different from the standard type of floor construction then in vogue. The three parts, front section, centre/rear wheel arch section, and rear section, when bolted together constituted a single raft. This complete floor was mounted to the chassis on rubber anti-vibration pick ups, which in turn allowed complete freedom of movement between chassis and body. This method of body mounting absorbed the major high velocity deflections from the chassis, which had been known to rapidly weaken traditional bodies mounted rigidly to the chassis when operated over poor road surfaces.

When the prototype was run over 5,000 miles round the army test track it was done with the floor traps removed, and the variation in deflection between body and chassis was readily apparent to the naked eye. The floor framing was fabricated from rolled-drawn carbon-steel, with mild steel sections. The panelling was aluminium alloy, and the underside was bonded to a bitumen impregnated felt matting to provide protection from corrosion and offer a degree of soundproofing. Non-corrodible chequer-plate extended some distance up the side of the body, and formed a triangular bracket offering both strengthening and stress-relieving properties.

Top Left: *The interior of an Almet bus, with European seating, destined for Gibralta.*

Centre Right: *The prototype Almet was proved by running it for 5,000 miles round the British military vehicle testing ground, on a course designed to duplicate the worst possible conditions that military vehicles were likely to encounter. The rugged durability of the Almet attracted a large number of customers, especially in those countries where the road infrastructure was not at its best. Africa, the Indian continent and the middle-east were all highly successful markets. This particular model was exported to an oil company in Kuwait at the beginning of 1950, and features protective louvres on the window openings.*

Bottom Right: *It is terrible to say that dual entrance buses were often the accepted practice in countries where racial discrimination was applied. It seemed that black and white people might travel in the same bus, but they had to use separate doors. This bus for the Overseas Motor Transport Co. (Uganda) has the dual entrance Type-A Almet body, with eight first class (upholstered) seats, and 20 second (slatted) seats. Note the chequer-plate aluminium floor.*

Top Left: *This stunning example of coachbuilding showed just what Duple could turn out for the export market. Unlike the 38-39 'native' buses with their basic longitudinal slatted seats, this attractive OB , with centre entrance, had just 10 seats. It was built for the Overseas Motor Transport Co., and intended for long distance tours in East Africa. A large capacity luggage area was accessed either internally, or via a drop-down boot, The body was constructed from special aluminium, which was mounted on to selected timers that were designed to withstand the vagaries of both tropical climates and insect attack. The roof and windscreen were all fixed, but the side windows were of the full-drop type. Roof ventilators and electric fans were fitted to offer maximum comfort. The livery was pale battleship grey, with green trip.*

Centre Left: *The interior of the OB coach seen above. Note the aircraft type seats are made from lightweight dural tubing and upholstered in grey leather. Each seat had a magazine/parcel pocket, and could be adjusted to suit the comfort of the First Class passenger whilst travelling in Africa.*

Bottom Left: *One of a batch of three OBs supplied to Gibralta Motorways, carrying chassis numbers 19281, 19284 or 19285. This picture was found in the Vauxhall archive with a note accompanying it saying, the Almet was shortly to be phased out in favour of the new Duple MkIV service bus.*

The body structure of the Almet was comprised of several units, namely the roof, rear dome unit, front screen unit, and the nearside and offside panels. However, to facilitate different entrances and door positions, there was variation in the nearside and offside panels. These panels were again variable, depending on whether the bus was to be fitted with either a single entry door, or a dual entry layout. In addition internal panels were supplied.

The framing consisted of steel sections, bolted together at main points with any sub-assemblies welded or rivetted in place. The side panels were locked to the pillars by special cover strips, but these were easily removed to replace damaged panels. Generally 18swg aluminium was used for all panelling, except for the rear dome unit and rear three quarters, which were produced from 18swg steel to give greater rigidity to the assembly. All the interior panels were made from 20swg aluminium. Between internal and external panels, the void was partially filled with a sound-deadening material to prevent 'drumming'. However, a 2-inch (51mm) gap was left for cooling purposes. The roof was double-skinned and filled with a layer of heat insulating material, this absorbed and diffused heat in hot countries and provided insulation in cold ones.

A roof luggage container was available as an optional extra, as was the rear ladder required to reach the container or roof rack. This container acted as another stress-absorbing member, and was rated as having a 1/4-ton (254kg) capacity but in many countries service agents reported that the racks were being seriously overloaded.

All the electrical wiring within each panel was a separate circuit, and could be joined to the electrical system by means of simple connectors. Lights, fittings etc, all came within the equipment packs, as did seats, hand rails etc.

There was a choice of internal specifications, and the buyer could select from a variety of layouts, any of which were suitable for left-hand or right-hand drive. For the MkI or MkII body, there was five options namely, 30-seats European type, 28-seats (8 1st class, 20 2nd class), 39-seats native type, 38-seats, and 20 seats (8 1st, 12 2nd) plus luggage compartment. For the MkIII or MkIV body there was only a 31-seat European type body. Finally the MkV and MkVI had the choice of a 30-seat European body, or a 29-seat European (semi-luxury type body.)

We have no way of telling just how many Almets were built, or how many OB chassis were supplied for the Almets. There is a distinct possibility that the number may be greater than many people envisage, as recent events have shown vehicles recorded as being exported with Duple service bus bodies, were in fact fitted with Almet bodies. The Almet seems to have been phased out in the latter part of the 1940s, but we know that CKD kits were still being supplied in some countries as late as 1952. In the early 1950s the OB's successor, the SB was fitted with an export body called the Metsec, but none of the records I have consulted have shown this to have been a widely successful venture. The much-needed metal framing therefore seems to have died a death at Duple until the introduction of the new Duple Dominant in 1972.

Top Right: *Duple were not alone in building all-metal bodies, and another serious contender in this field was the Southampton firm of Sparshatt. Their body came in ten sections and fitted in a packing case 96 inches x 124 inches x 82 inches (2.43m x 3.15m x 2.8m). They claimed that it took just 100 man-hours to erect. This example is seen on 14th January 1949 at Southampton docks in front of the new Cunard-White Star liner the RMS Caronia. Built by John Brown on Clydeside and launched in October 1947, the Caronia sported a two-tone pale green livery which imparted the nickname, 'The Green Goddess'. Sold off by Cunard in 1967 the ship worked cruises from New York to the Caribbean. She sank off the island of Guam in the Pacific, whilst en-route to a breaker's yard in 1974.*

Centre Right: *This esoteric OB carries a body by Belgian builders Van Hool. The Van Hool carried 36 passengers, and cost a substantial £2,000 (or around £32,882 today), and was significantly more than Duple's Vista which was then selling in Europe at £1,275 (£20,962). This example is seen at the Brussels Motor Show. However, notice the width of the body over the wheels.*

Bottom Right: *Taken by the Foreign Vehicle Section of the Ministry of Supply, this picture shows a very elegant-looking OB. There is no record of which British firm built the 34-seater coach for the Belgian firm of Continental Automobile Tourism.*

THE POST-WAR OB

The autumn of 1945 saw Vauxhall's production facilities stretched to capacity and, with every chassis being sold before it was built, it may be thought that there was little point in the company actively promoting new sales. With the massive export sales programme accounting for the bulk of new chassis, there was a huge demand for the remaining production and almost any chassis could be sold here in Britain.

Such was the shortage of new chassis, that large numbers of ex-military and utility vehicles were bought by bus operators and re-bodied to meet the rapidly emerging demand for public travel. Some unusual vehicles appeared in this time, including a number of Bedford QLs. The 4x4 configuration of the QL made it ideal for difficult terrain, and one user was Southport Corporation who used QLs to provide services out along the expanse of sand at this Lancashire seaside resort. In many operations it was 'make do and mend', but it is quite clear that a boom time was ahead.

The first milestone came in September 1945, when the Ministry of War Transport wrote to Vauxhall, and advised them that the need for a 'License to Acquire' would be revoked at midnight on 31st December. Knowing that many firms would take this opportunity to place orders for extra vehicles, even if they were not readily available, Vauxhall began a new marketing strategy for the OB.

The OWB remained in production, but it was to be progressively phased out. The official partnership was still with Duple, and the 1946 OB catalogue (produced in October 1945) offered a choice of two bodies. These were the Vista Luxury Coach, with built-in luggage locker, sliding roof and parcel racks. It was offered in three seating capacities 26 (four-passenger rear seat), 27 (five-passenger rear seat) and 29-seat. The prices ranged from £1,265 (£23,750) to £1,275 (£23,938), whilst for £1,140 (£21,403) buyers could acquire the new 32-seat MkII service bus. With the introduction of the MkII, Vauxhall entered an agreement with Duple and Mulliners that, as new OBs came on stream, the remaining OWBs would be sent to Birmingham rather than Hendon for bodying.

Top Left: *As mentioned later in this chapter, the OB was really the true rural bus, and it could handle both major roads and country lanes with equal equanimity. Few British roads at the time could have been testing as those in the far north of Scotland, and with the exception of the Shetland Islands you can not get much further north than the Orkneys. Here we see a 1946 OB with the SMT Vista body after delivery to John G. Nicholson of Stromness, Orkney. Registered BS 2268, and with Tom Drever at the wheel, the Vista runs past the Movement Control office on the pier at Stromness, whilst the freighter ss St. Ola is seen in the background.*

Top Right: *This view clearly shows the OB chassis and the double drop arrangement that gave the coach its low floor height. This represents the final OB chassis and dates from the summer of 1949. The illustration is also very useful in the fact that it shows the way in which the prop-shaft split into two sections, with the rear part connecting to the offset differential on the off-side of the rear axle. For anyone who has ever worked under an old Bedford bus chassis, then gone home and filled the bottom of the bath with copious amounts of rusty metal flakes, the sight of such a pristine chassis is truly a joy to behold.*

Bottom Right: *Another example of the type of route on which the OB excelled is shown in this superb view of AEP 551 at Dolau. In the fleet of Mid-Wales Motorways, Newtown, Montgommeryshire, the Vista is seen on 28th December 1950 heading for Mochdre.*

The construction specification for the Vista included framing with selected timber, which was reinforced with steel at all stressed points. It also had a sliding panel roof and stainless capped intermediate pillars. The floor was 3/4-inch (19mm) tongue and grooved boards, screwed to the framing. A raised seat floor allowed a gangway that deepened as it progressed to the rear of the coach, and access traps in the floor were metal edged. The sliding entrance door returned, but this time on the outside of the panelling, rather than sliding inside the body as had been the case on the pre-war OB. An emergency exit was located on the off-side of the vehicle, between the driver's seat and the first pair of passenger seats on that side.

The driver's cab had a vee sloping front, with a metal-framed two-panel screen on the driver's side; the driver's screen could be opened for ventilation. The driver's seat was now fashioned with a leather covering, as opposed to the basic canvas seat cover that had been used throughout the war years. The passenger seats were made on Dean tubular frames, and had spring cushions and padded squabs covered in moquette trimmed with leather. Leather could be specified if required, whilst seat backs were either repp or leather. Ventilation was provided by breathers in all cavities, an air extractor mounted in the roof at the rear of the bus, and seven full-drop side windows. Electric equipment included nine pillar lamps and a rear dome with two bulbs. An electric bell or buzzer was provided near the driver, and three pushes were situated in the roof of the coach saloon.

Top Left: *British European Airways ran a modest sized fleet of OBs, mostly with Vista bodies by either Duple or SMT, they also had two 28-seat SMT Service Buses and two 32-seat Duple Service Buses. But nothing I have seen in print indicates that they had any of the 1948-9 Service Coaches. Yet here we see OMP 248 with a SMT Service Coach body, which has been reduced to 22-seats and given full height rear doors to form a large luggage locker. To add extra confusion, the picture carries a Duple body number and their official stamp!*

Centre Left: *Mind you photographs are not always what they seem, as we see from this photograph taken at Whitby, where fake sky has been added (note the difference of the sky through the coach windows with that over the roof. The SMT Vista, KUA 186, is working one of Wallace Arnold's regular tours from Leeds to Whitby, Scarborough or Filey on the Yorkshire coast.*

Bottom Left: *Another SMT offering, featuring the earlier style Vista body (internal sliding door) on BJT 894. It is seen here in the fleet of Bere Regis & District on the 20th January 1948. The legal lettering on the side shows it was licensed to carry 27 passengers at a maximum speed of 30mph.*

The specification for the MkII Service Bus was quite similar to the Vista, but the framing was a mixture of hardwood and steel flitches, plates and gussets. The roof was made from ash, but steel tie-plates were also used. The seats were more austere than in the Vista, but again there was a choice of leather or moquette and leather. Ten interior lights (with Diffusalite glass shades) provided internal illumination. Oddly, the destination blind only came with the word 'Private', which contrasted with the six free names provided on the Vista.

The chassis itself cost £440 (£8,824), and its proven reliability and economy began to attract a large number of other coach-builders. By trawling through the records, it has emerged that over 60 British firms were to body the OB in the next five years, although a few (like J. H. Jennings of Sandbach, Wilson & Stockall of Bury and Vincents of Reading) also produced commercial bodies like horseboxes, travelling banks or mobile libraries. Around 52 coachbuilders seem to have acquired new OB chassis purely for coaches, but once again many of these firms did not make any major contribution to the bus and coach scene, and some only bodied one or two examples.

The evidence on who built what is far from conclusive, and at this stage it would be imprudent to try and quote a list of builders. However, of the better known names building coaches or service buses on the OB, we can mention firms like Arlington, Barnaby, Beadle, Burlingham, Challenger, Churchill, Duple, Gurney Nutting, Man Egerton, Marshall, Mulliner, Pearson, Plaxton, Portsmouth Aviation, Kennings, Lee Motors, Reeves, Roe, SMT, Scottish Aviation, Sparshatt, Strachan, Thurgood, Trans-United, Willenhall, Woodall Nicholson, and Yeates.

With the contributions of these coachbuilders, allied to the efforts of Duple, the OB went on to assume a significant role in the development of the British bus and coach industry in the five years that followed World War II. Not only did the OB become the chosen vehicle of the small operator, but many larger concerns chose it as an adequate means of reinforcing or supplementing their fleets. Even the BET and Tilling companies bought significant numbers of OBs, even though some (like Southdown) only acquired them for use on routes where heavier coaches were either prohibited or uneconomical. Competition in the same field came from the Austin CXB and the Commer Commando, but the OWB/OB sold in the thousands, and neither Austin or Commer came anywhere near this.

Standardisation was the main goal of the Bedford-Duple alliance, but even within this objective there were many variations. One significant order was from the Nottinghamshire firm of Barton Transport, who ordered a number of 24-seat Vistas, and had these fitted with reclining seats and perspex roof panels.

Another group of vehicles supplied with non-standard Vista bodies were five coaches to United Services Transport Co., for use on their contract to KLM Royal Dutch Airlines. As the picture below shows, these coaches also had just 24 seats, and a huge boot with full-height doors occupied the rear of the bus. The OB was also popular with other airlines, and used by them both at home and abroad. Included in this list was BOAC, BEA, Malayan Airlines, Quantas, Sabena and the Ministry of Civil Aviation. In addition they were also used as airport buses by civil undertakings at London, Liverpool and Glasgow to name but three.

Top Right: *Although not a service bus in the true sense of the word, this OB carries the Duple MkIV Service Bus body. Provided with 30-seats, it was operated by Fisons Limited, Ipswich and used to carry workers to and from the company's fertiliser works at Immingham, in North Lincolnshire.*

Centre Right: *As will be noted from other pictures in the book, OBs were quite popular on airport services. The majority were of course operated by the airlines themselves, but in this September 1956 view we see OMX 356 leaving Liverpool's Speke Airport. Operated by the Liverpool Corporation Passenger Transport Department, in which it was fleet number B4, the OB carries a 1948-9 Duple Service Coach body. Note however, the normal side guard rail has been replaced by a full panel skirt.*

Bottom Right: *Following a number of diversions from one airport to another in the foggy London winter of 1946-7, KLM contracted United Services Transport to provide 'transfer coaches'. These were to be used for connections in bad weather, and a scheduled service from various airports into central London at other times. The 24-seat coaches again featured full-height rear doors and a large luggage locker, but unlike the BEA coach this was separated from the main saloon by a full-height bulkhead.*

Top Left: *In this selection of photographs, we show the interior of the Vista coach. In this 1948 view of a Greenslades Vista, the driver's 'cab' is well illustrated with all the controls clearly visible. The unusual feature is the 'counter' showing 'five' on the bulkhead. This was a device that Greenslades employed in conjunction with a printed itinerary given to the passengers. Each time a new point of interest was reached on a tour, the driver would activate the cable control on the dash to change the number and ring the bell.*

Centre & Bottom Left: *What may well be the interior of the first post-war Vista Luxury coach to leave the Hendon works. (Look through the windscreen of the coach and note all the OWBs in production inside the factory.) The coach itself has tubular framed seats and an internal sliding door, but no clock!*

The 1947 Bedford Duple catalogue was published in October 1946 and showed little change to the previous brochure, except the price of the Vista (now advertised as 27 or 29 seats) was £1,415 (£26,566) and £1,425 (£26,754) and the 32-seat MkII Service Bus was listed at £1,290 (£24,219). Yet by the start of 1947 these prices had increased to £1,460 (£27,411), £1,470 (£27,599) and £1,315 (£24,689) respectively, whilst the service bus was reduced in capacity to 31 seats. A change was noted in the ratio of the full floating rear axle, which went from 6.16:1 to 5.86:1, and the chassis price increased to £440 (£8,261) ex-works.

In September 1948 Vauxhall sent its customers this notice: 'Recent Government directives suggested that production of 'Vista' coaches would have to stop at once. It has now been agreed, however, that existing stocks of materials may be used up on luxury coachwork, and production of this body will continue until mid-November.' By the time that the November 1948 brochure was produced, the Vista no longer appeared. In its place Duple advertised the 27- and 29-seat MkV service coach at £1,473-£1,483 (£27,655-£27,843) respectively. It was, in essence, very little different to the Vista and the only immediate feature was the omission of the distinctive side flash carried on the Vista. Internally Duple had been forced to dispense with the sprung seat, as the concept of luxury travel did not sit well with the Government in what was considered a period of austerity. Furthermore, on the instructions of the Ministry, the sliding roof, clock and bulkhead mirrors were also withdrawn.

For service vehicles, the MkIV made its appearance at £1,423 (£26,716) with a capacity of 29- or 30-seats, and 31-seats in the export version. Both the service coach and the service bus enjoyed minor refinements that had not been included in the earlier post-war buses, and even roof-linings began to reappear. The chassis itself was now £508 (£9.537). One worrying factor in the OWBs built after the end of 1943, was the fact that the poorer quality of timber used in construction, was now beginning to lead to body-sag. Therefore, to overcome this problem, and also help operators get around supply restrictions, Duple offered to re-body existing chassis provided they were thoroughly overhauled by a Vauxhall dealer first.

In April 1949, however, the *Bedford Transport Magazine* announced, 'Lifting of Government restrictions imposed on coach building about the middle of last year means that the Bedford Vista coach can go back into production again.' A new pressed-alloy seat frame was introduced, and Dunlopillo latex cushions made a welcome re-appearance now that rubber restrictions had been lifted. Formica appeared on the side panels as an included item, as did anodised vent grills and wood veneer on the bulkhead. This led to the withdrawal of the MkV Service Coach, and although a few were made up from remaining components, its production life was very short.

A Radiomobile system could be supplied with speakers for £55.10s (£1,042), or as a complete radio/public address system at £60.10s (£1,127). A Clayton heater would cost £37.10s (£704) extra, and cant rail roof windows were available, four each side, at £30 (£563) extra. The MkIV Service Bus had increased in price to £1,475 (£27,693) and specification stayed pretty much as they had been in 1948, although Formica again made an appearance. Mind you the number of bell-pushes dwindled to just two (one front, one rear) but buyers did get six names on the destination blind. By the time that the final OB catalogue was issued by Vauxhall in October 1949, the Vista cost £1,634 (££30,678) for the 27-seater and £1,645 (£30,884) for the 29-seater. The last price listed for the MkV Service Bus was £1,475 (£27,693) but the OB chassis was still £580 (£10,989).

As will be expected with such a large number of OBs being produced, the variety of vehicles operating in Britain was quite wide. As stated earlier, even firms who had operated a 'big bus' policy before the war found themselves with OWBs or OBs in their fleet after it. In a number of cases these acquisitions were purely out of necessity rather than choice, but once acquired the little Bedfords began to prove their worth. Firms like Wallace Arnold of Leeds, found that the small buses were ideal for tour work, and their economy of operation offset the loss of seating capacity.

Top Right: *As will be appreciated, the bulk of the photographs in this book show Bedford-Duple combinations, because the Vauxhall archive reflects the 'official' build policy. However, we have already shown SMT, who built the Vista body under licence, but we should not ignore Plaxtons of Scarborough. Here we see one of their semi-forward control OBs with a full-front body on FHP 782. Along with th AEC Regal-Windover coach next to, the OB was in the fleet of Brown's of Caistor (Lincolnshire).*

Centre Right: *A few miles to the north, Leon's of Finningley used this Plaxton-bodied OB (KRR 990) on services into South Yorkshire and North Lincolnshire.*

Bottom Right: *The Vauxhall archive is unclear on the type of body used on GJW 683, but the general consensus of opinion is that it carries a Mulliner body. It was one of two such coaches employed by Keele University in Staffordshire.*

Top Left: *The next example we see features a Thurgood Touring Coach. Built for Hillside Garages, this OB has the 20-seat continental luxury touring body complete with specially adjustable seats that gave a semi-reclining position. Turned out in 1949, KRO 672 was the 208th Thurgood Continental Tourer.*

Centre Left: *In the heart of the Pennines, Keighley-West Yorkshire provided several services up steep rugged hillsides. One such route was the Keighley - Riddlesden route, which included steep banks, hairpin bends, and a bridge with a 3-ton load limit and just seven inches clearance for an OB. No wonder it had route number 13. To work the route, Keighley-West Yorkshire asked J. C. Beadle to build two special bodies to meet the stringent criteria. Here FFX 550 turns a blind corner into Ilkley Road.*

Bottom Left: *For export airline use, we see a left-hand drive OB with a Churchill 27-seat rear-entry body for BOAC.*

The profitability of the Bedford bus chassis was clearly recognised by other large firms, and some of them decided to standardise entirely on the OB. One example is the firm of Bere Regis & District Transport, who had depots in Bere Regis, Blandford and Dorchester. The firm ran a large number of stage carriage services, but they also undertook a great deal of excursion and tour work especially in the summer season. By the summer of 1947 the company was operating a total of 62 Bedfords, the oldest of which was a 1933 WHL. On average each coach clocked up around 40,000 miles every year, as the firm were achieving around two and a half million miles per annum.

One of the new OB Vistas that was put into service in May 1946, achieved a total of 75,000 miles by the end of April 1947; an aggregate of almost 1,500 miles a week. Reliability, efficiency and presentation was ensured by the fact that the firm had a policy where each driver had his 'own' coach and was responsible for its upkeep. One driver so loved his rural route that he inveigled his father, the local parson, to come and help him as a part-time conductor - presumably on the basis that he was used to conducting services!

Another southern firm who used Bedfords were the Exeter company of Greenslades, a name that will be familiar with hundreds of holiday-makers who travelled to the south-west in the post-war years. Their popular tours along the Devon coast and their 'English Switzerland Trip' (Lynton, Lynmouth and Minehead) made great use of the attractive new Vista coaches, whilst OWBs and OB service buses were also prominent in the fleet.

Up in the Pennines, the firm of Baddeley Brothers, who used to run my school bus service, were serving the down to earth Yorkshiremen. The town in which they were based, Holmfirth, had yet to achieve fame as the setting for the TV series Last of The Summer Wine and tourism was associated only with weekend or summer evening trips into the nearby Peak District or Yorkshire Dales. As a boy I recall the firm had OWBs EWT 653 (SMT), EWU 394, EWX 438 and ENX 113 (Duple), and ERM 533 (Cressbank).

In 1946 Baddeley's ordered two more OBs, one with a Duple MKII Service Bus body and one with a Plaxton coach body, that were to be registered FWR 32-3 respectively. However, problems in supply meant that Bedford could not offer two chassis, and at the last minute Plaxton found a Commer Commando for the coach body. The Bedfords worked mostly on the firm's three stage carriage routes, contract work, or school runs. But I recall that when we used to take evening mystery trips, or a trip to Castleton in the Peak District, the Bedfords were usually turned out, mind you they creaked, rattled and rolled all the way over Holme Moss and down to Glossop.

Several operators also bodied their own OB chassis, and the firm of Scottish Motor Traction springs readily to mind. Another of the firms listed earlier, Trans United Coachcraft of Rochdale, were owned by a consortium of coach companies, including Yelloways of Oldham. Ironically, all the OBs used by Yelloways for holiday and tour work had Duple bodies.

Another firm bodying OB chassis was Black & White Coaches of Walthamstow, who claimed to be the first to fit fluorescent lights in a motor coach. The technique had been developed by CAV at the end of 1945, who installed an experimental system in a Nottingham Corporation bus. The difficulties of powering fluorescent tubes is fully described in the September 1948 issue of the *Bedford Transport Magazine*, along with a series of interesting illustrations. The article pointed out that the system was installed in a 1946 OB Vista, and the vehicle re-entered service in June 1947, after which it did 16,000 miles in active use prior to the article declaring that the system had been thoroughly tested. By the summer of 1948, four Black & White Vistas had been equipped, including MPU 61. The firm also offered to convert OBs for other operators, the cost being £100 (£1,877) and not the £170 (£3,191) quoted in other publications.

Top Right: *This trio of illustrations serve to show the difference between the normal control Bedford OB chassis, and the forward control type. In the top picture we see the cab layout of a 1945 OWB, with the steering position on a normal link down to the front axle, and the bonnet of the vehicle extending beyond the windscreen. Note that the chassis has just clocked up 52 miles, presumably in factory testing and the delivery to Hendon.*

Centre Right: *The benefit of forward control was that it gave more space inside the body, either for extra seating or for wider spacing between the seats. In view of the regulations on the number that could be carried, those firms who opted for forward or semi-forward control, often did so to achieve more passenger leg room. This unusual half-cab version of the OB, KOM 404 from 1950, was supplied to A.V. Page of Great Barr, Birmingham. with 31 seats.*

Bottom Right: *This chassis was built in October 1946 for testing and evaluation; note the forward control position, with linkage leading back to the front axle. This particular chassis was bodied by Willenhall and became URE 262 in the fleet of Bennetts of Fraddon.*

Another London operator with a large fleet of Bedfords, were Orange Luxury Coaches of Kennington. By the end of 1947 they had 50 Bedfords, the oldest of which were 1937 WLBs. Supplemented with OWBs and an increasing fleet of Vista-bodied OBs, the fleet were completing a combined figure of 1,250,000 miles each year and some buses were doing daily trips of 250 or 300 miles a day on the firm's express services. Not a lot by today's standard, but on the twisting, winding roads of the day, runs to Bournemouth, Great Yarmouth, and even Brighton often meant that average speed was no more than 20mph. In 1947 the fleet of Vistas carried 140,000 passengers, and did so in complete reliability, as it was the policy of Orange Coaches to operate without a reserve vehicle in the fleet.

Yet, it was not just the big operators who used the OWB and OB in that post-war period, and it remained very much at the heart of the rural bus business. I could cite hundreds of examples where small operators made substantial profits from their little Bedfords!

I could also print a long list of 'one-man-band' businesses but I am going to cite an example of one small operator, and in this I rely on my good friend Gordon Jamieson from the Isle of Yell in the Shetlands. As the reader will have noted, we have used a few pictures of Shetland Bedfords in this book, and the reason is quite simply that Trans-Pennine are producing a definitive history of *Shetland Island Buses In The 20th Century*, written by Gordon. He recalls:-

'Our first bus was a Chevrolet, but the first Bedford we bought was a 1935 WLB, which we acquired in 1948 and ran as a PSV until 1953. When its bus service days were over the body was cut off to leave a chassis cowl, and we fitted it with a flat bed body (open cab) for use on our farm. Another small Bedford dating from 1939, a WS Type with 14-seats, was purchased from MacBraynes to replace it.

Our first OB was purchased in 1955 from Hutchesons of Dundee (YJ 8939), at the relatively young age of 8 years old. It had a Plaxton 27-seat body, a crash gear box and ordinary control. It was the largest vehicle on the Isle of Yell at the time, and we operated it until 1972. This was bus on which I passed my test on in 1968, but it had an ignominious end; first becoming a mobile fish and chip van, and later became a peat shed until it was cleared away 1996. At the same time we had another OB, this time a 1950 Mulliner bodied MkII service bus (PS 1999). We purchased it in 1960 and scrapped it in 1969.

Around this time there were four other OBs on Yell. The were all very reliable, really economical, very simple to drive and it was easy to learn how to maintain them. We kept the crash boxes on our OBs, but the other local firm (Mansons of West Sandwick) fitted theirs with synchromesh boxes. The last OBs ran in Yell back in 1977, when they were traded into the Moseley group. They intended to restore these at the time, but for various reasons this did not take place then. However ERG 164 is now being restored in South Yorkshire. Another preservation scheme is underway for SL 3474, which was also taken out of service in 1977. Two more Shetland OBs went in 1979; HE 219 for preservation, whilst LSM 44 became a greenhouse. These these were the last OBs operated in the Shetlands, but LSM 44 still exists in a derelict state, and the basis for a potential preservation scheme.

Both Pages: *For those readers who are also interested in railways, this series of pictures will be of undoubted interest, as it shows one of British Railways O-Type buses. Many readers will know that British Railways had quite a few OWB /OB buses and coaches in their fleet, especially in the south west, East Anglia and Scotland. Other firms, including the Scottish Co-operative Society operated services on behalf of BR with OBs. The bulk of BR's Bedfords were bodied by Duple or SMT, but we have discovered that there was at least one Plaxton (used by the Signalling & Telegraph Department at York), and two Mulliner OWBs (used by the Permanent Way Department of the Western Region in Wales). One supplier who provided at least three types of Bedford coach to British Railways between 1948 and 1950 was All-Weather Motor Bodies of Maida Vale. Yet, in the list of builders shown in the book detailing the OB and OWB, this firm does not appear. Yet, as far as I can tell from BR records, All-Weather produced numerous bodies for the national rail network. In the case of KXU 332, which was used as a 'Special Private Train Crew Bus', All-Weather employed the OLAZ chassis and OB springing. As will be appreciated the OLAZ was primarily a goods vehicle chassis, but it served the purpose that many operators still required for their existing work. In this selection of photographs the OLAZ-All-Weather combination is demonstrated from every conceivable angle, and hopefully this may prompt a few 'railway modellers' to have a go at producing an interesting model for their layout. The BR fleet number was S237W and had the body number G4454 allocated. G4455 was also recorded as All-Weather, and at least five more followed this pair. Further details on British Railway road coaches and crew buses would be gratefully welcomed. Readers may like to know that there is a book in the **Nostalgia Road** series entitled British Railways Road Vehicles 1948-1968, along with books on Great Western Railway and LMS Railway road vehicles.*

Top Left: *As stated previously, the OLAZ provided a stop-gap filler between the OB and the SB, at least until Bedford-Duple could begin to market a 27- to 29-seat bus again. In fact it would do this a few years later when the 29-seat Bella-Vista emerged to meet the needs of the smaller capacity bus operator in the early 1960s. As the co-owner of a Bella Vista, I could say an awful lot more on this subject, but readers will have to wait until our next book in the **Fare Stage Series**, Bedford Buses in the 1950s and '60s. Meantime, here we see OLAZ MXV 578 with the Sportsman demonstrator body at Farnborough on 8th July 1952.*

Centre Left: *The light, stylish and attractive interior of a 1952 'Sportsman', including netted luggage racks. However, according to the information written on the rear of this picture, this coach carries a different body number to that placed on MXV 578. Whether this indicates that a second body was completed, or is merely a clerical error, I can not say.*

Bottom Left: *On a Kentish tour, the OLAZ Sportsman , calls at The Blue Boys public house for a 'refreshment' stop. This typical period picture is complemented by the grain stores and oast house .*

The demise of the OB and its replacement with the 33-seat SB (the Big Bedford) left a gap in the market that still had to be filled. Many operators expressed a demand for a 26- to 29-seat coach, and several wrote to Bedford making their feelings abundantly clear. Obviously this resistance to the SB was neither universal, nor long-lasting, but it did prompt discussions between Vauxhall and Duple. A few OB chassis were still in the pipe-line, but OB was officially ended in October 1950. As the O and M type goods vehicles were to remain in production until 1953, these could be made available to operators or coachbuilders who wanted to build buses in the 14- to 27-seat range. One such operator was the Scottish firm of David MacBrayne who ordered a batch of service buses on the OLAZ lorry chassis.

The demand for smaller buses declined even further when the SB began to demonstrate that it could be carry 33 passengers just as economically as could be carried in the 29-seat OB. In a final fling to promote the 3-ton chassis, Bedford and Duple built their FS50 'Sportsman' body. This featured a unique external framing, which imitated the 'shooting brake or station wagon' style that was very much in fashion in the early 1950s. In all three types of "Sportsman' body were designed, two to fit the OLAZ and one to fit the M-Type. The M Type and one OLAZ body were completed, and the second was at least commenced. The one OLAZ that we know to have been finished went to Lewis coaches at Farnborough, Kent.

In conclusion we should mention that the OB specifications varied little over the production years, although many minor improvements were made. The desire for diesel engines that was seen elsewhere in the bus and coach industry never really challenged the economical petrol OB, but some had Perkins P6 diesel engines fitted during production or as 'dealer-fitted' replacements.

During their service lives operators were known to fit other makes of engine, and Austin-Morris, Ford, and Gardner diesel engines are all known to have been used. Both diesel and petrol engines were used on non-PSV OB applications, where a variety of body-builders offered a wide selection of special constructions. Most of these were used as vehicles where the low floor height of the bus chassis was more suited to the particular application than were the conventional O-Type lorry chassis. Examples were horseboxes, travelling libraries, mobile shops, 'black marias' (prison vans), cattle vans, travelling banks, display and advertising units, mobile cafes and even fish & chip shops. In their after life several OBs and OWBs were converted into similar non-PSV uses, and I vividly recall the OB that my Uncle John used as a travelling green-grocers shop in the Colne Valley of Huddersfield.

Yet, just as the PSV chassis was used for commercial application, commercial chassis were used in PSV application. In discussing the OLAZ and the earlier goods vehicles bodied as coaches, we have given some idea about the endless possibilities of the O-Type at large. Yet we have not discussed the final application, namely in the Bedford-Scammell OSS tractor unit, which was used to pull trailer coaches. The trend began with ex-military OXC units and trailers which were converted by Dysons, British Trailer Co. (BTC), and Roe to provide 44- to 50-seat mass-transit coaches (for internal use at airports, factories and dockyards etc.), mobile canteens, and even television studios. None of these were allowed on the public highway, as 'buses', because their 30-foot (9.1m) length and 101-inch (2.56m) width made them well above the legal maximum for use on the public highway. Two were operated by Liverpool Corporation in connection with armaments factories during the war, and one was used in South Wales at a similar establishment. However, after the war the new OSS 'buses' were strictly limited to 'off-road' applications.

Top Right: *In 1946 several mass-transit bodies became available from war-work applications, and a number of municipal undertakings looked at the possibility of using this type of 'bus' to provide public services. However Construction & Use regulations prevented this, but the units did have future possibilities in public transport applications, ranging from mobile ticket offices, staff canteens, travelling 'classrooms', and even health-care units. This use of ex-wartime vehicles led to 'new build' in the years that followed. Here we see a December 1955 view of a London Transport staff canteen behind OSS tractor JXC 1.*

Centre Right: *This 1950 view shows the bus station in the Shotton steel works of John Summers & Sons. Here BTC units and OSS tractors form a mass transit system that perambulated the works, linking local PSV services with the various departments in the steel works. Summers had at least 10 of these units.*

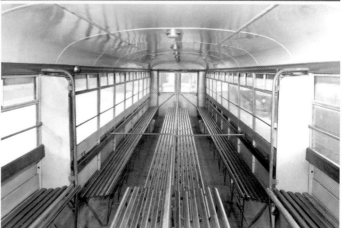

Bottom Right: *A rare internal view of one of the Shotton BTC trailer units - move down the bus, plenty of room inside!*

It is always difficult to reach this point in a book, because so much has been left unsaid. There is always the thought that you have missed out something important, and even made an error or two. Yet in producing this work, I have been aided by a magnificent collection of official records at the Luton works of Vauxhall Motors. This has been supplemented by the wonderful collection of Vauxhall photographs. I am therefore deeply indebted to Peter Blincow, Ray Cooper, Stuart Harris, David Hine and Dennis Sherer, for their kind assistance and also to John Ankerman and Barry Harvey of the Vauxhall, Bedford Opel Owners Association for their encouragement. In addition, I have been greatly helped by Mike Berry, Brian Duncan and Gordon Jamieson, who between them had the onerous task of deciding which of the magnificent pictures to use and which to omit.

I should also thank both Robert Berry and Mike Fenton for checking the manuscript, and for the encouragement of Jeff Colledge, Brian Gooding, and Philip Lamb who all told me to get on and produce a much needed book. But, that said any mistakes herein are mine and mine alone. I also want to thank Richard Haughey and the people at Dews Coaches for hosting the launch of this book at the Bedford Gathering in August 2000.

Above. *This was one of a pair of 1948 OB chassis obtained in a deal by David Brown Tractors of Huddersfield, who traded tractors with Vauxhalls for the chassis. The bodies were by Woodall & Nicholson, and registered HWT 628-9 at Wakefield in 1948.*

The fact that so much material has emerged, and that quite a few accepted views have been challenged does not take anything away from what has been written before, and I would thank the earlier authors who have touched on this subject and stimulated my interest in Bedford buses and coaches. I hope that you have enjoyed the images we selected, and I trust that you will read the two follow-on books in this series, one covering *Bedford Buses in the 1950s and '60s*, and one covering *Bedford Buses in the 1970s and '80s*.

Finally, those who are interested in helping to preserve old Bedford buses, may like to become a supporter of the Viking Coach Trust, who are currently engaged in saving and restoring a number of Bedfords. Both active and armchair support is actively welcomed, and details are available from the publishers. In this way, you too can help turn frozen images from books like this into a real piece of transport history on which people can still travel. If you agree, why not contact the Trust care of Trans-Pennine Publishing.